BALL CANNING BOOK 2023 FOR BEGINNERS

Easy Guide to Unlock the Art of Preserving With Ball Canning, the Trusted Brand for Canning Enthusiasts

LARRY J. WILLIAMS

Copyright © 2023 **Larry J. Williams**

All rights reserved. This book or any portion thereof may not be reproduced or used in any manner whatsoever without the express written permission of the publisher except for the use of brief quotations in a book review.

Printed in the United States of America

© **Larry J. Williams**

Table of Contents

CHAPTER 1 1
- Introduction to Ball Canning.. 1
- Definition and Purpose of Canning.. 8
- Importance of Ball Canning... 12
- Benefits of Ball Canning.. 13

CHAPTER 2 16
- Understanding Canning Basics 17
- Safety Guidelines and Precautions 19
- Equipment and Tools for Ball Canning 19
- Preparing Jars and Lids 23
- Canning Methods and Techniques 24

CHAPTER 3 25
- Water Bath Canning... 25
- Step-by-Step Guide to Water Bath Canning 26
- Method 1 26
- Method 2 29
- Preparing the Recipe 31
- Preparing Jars and Lids 37
- Filling Jars and Removing Air Bubbles 40
- Applying Lids and Processing Jars 44

Cooling, Storing, and Checking Seals 47

CHAPTER 4 51

Pressure Canning 51

Introduction to Pressure Canning 51

What is high-pressure canning? 55

A Step-by-Step Guide to Pressure-Canning: 60

Method 1 60

Method 2 61

Preparing the Recipe 64

Preparing Jars and Lids 68

Filling Jars and Removing Air Bubbles 71

CHAPTER 5 74

Pickling and Fermenting 74

Pickling Techniques and Tips 79

Fermentation Basics and Guidelines 82

Pickling and Fermentation Recipes 83

CHAPTER 6 85

Jams, Jellies, and Preserves 85

Introduction to Making Jams, Jellies, and Preserves 87

Basic Fruit Preserving Techniques 92

Creating Jams, Jellies, and Preserves with Pectin 95

Fruits with Low Pectin Levels 97

Special Jam and Jelly Recipes 98

CHAPTER 7 100

Salsas, Sauces, and Relishes 100

Tomato-Based Salsa Recipes 103

Fruit-Based Salsa Recipes 110

Sauce Recipes 112

Relish Recipes 117

CHAPTER 8 121

Introduction to Canning Meats and Soups 121

Canning Meat and Poultry 124

Canning Soups and Stews 126

Recipes for Canned Meats and Soups 131

CHAPTER 9 138

Canning Fruits and Vegetables 138

Canning Fruits: Techniques and Recipes 143

Additional More Tips: 147

Canning Vegetables: Techniques and Recipes 148

Important Tips and Safety Precautions: 150

CHAPTER 10 152

Storing and Using Canned Goods 152

Section 1: Storing Canned Goods 152

Section 2: Using Canned Goods 153

Recipes and Meal Planning: 153

Factors that reduce the longevity of preserved foods. 154

Shelf life and best practices for storage 158

Understanding Factors Affecting the Shelf Life of Food Products 158

What is Food Shelf Life? 159

High-risk Foods 159

Low-risk Foods 160

What are the Factors Affecting Shelf Life? 161

How to Determine the Shelf Life of Food Products 164

How to Calculate Shelf Life 164

How to Increase the Shelf Life of Food Products 165

Methods for Increasing Shelf Life 166

Benefits of Extending Shelf Life 166

CONCLUSION 183

CHAPTER 1

Introduction to Ball Canning

Canning has been an age-old practice used by generations to preserve food, extend its shelf life, and savor the flavors of summer throughout the year. Among the various methods of food preservation, Ball canning stands out as a trusted and time-tested technique that has become synonymous with preserving freshness and flavor. Whether you're a seasoned canner or a novice looking to embark on this rewarding culinary journey, Ball canning offers a comprehensive range of tools, resources, and expertise to help you successfully preserve your harvest and create delicious homemade treats.

Ball, a renowned name in the canning industry, has a rich history dating back to the late 19th century. The Ball brothers, five siblings with a passion for innovation, set out to revolutionize food preservation by introducing a two-piece canning lid, the precursor to the modern-day canning jar lid we use today. This breakthrough invention brought a new level of convenience, safety, and reliability to home canning, making it more accessible and practical for households across the globe.

With over a century of expertise, Ball has continued to refine and expand its product line to meet the evolving needs of modern canners. From the iconic Ball Mason jars, available in a variety of sizes and designs, to state-of-the-art canning equipment and accessories, Ball offers a comprehensive range of products that cater to every canning requirement. These products are crafted with meticulous attention to detail and a commitment to quality, ensuring that your preserved foods stay fresh and flavorful for months or even years.

Moreover, Ball canning is not just about preservation—it's a celebration of self-sufficiency, sustainability, and the joy of creating homemade delicacies. By preserving your own food, you have control over the ingredients, ensuring that your family consumes wholesome, natural products without additives or preservatives. Additionally, canning allows you to reduce food waste, take advantage of seasonal abundance, and enjoy the fruits of your labor long after the harvest season has ended.

Ball canning is a trusted and respected name in the world of food preservation. With its rich history, high-quality products, and extensive resources, Ball empowers individuals to engage in the timeless art of canning. So, whether you're preserving your bountiful garden harvest, creating thoughtful homemade gifts, or simply seeking to embrace a more sustainable lifestyle, Ball canning provides the tools and knowledge to embark on a flavorful journey of self-sufficiency and culinary creativity.

Anyone can do it with some fundamental equipment, time, and a moderate amount of steam. Once you have mastered the skill, you will become addicted to it.

Canning maintains freshness.

Microorganisms and enzymes are inactivated when food vessels are heated at high temperatures for prolonged periods. Simultaneously, air is expelled from the vessels, resulting in a vacuum seal.

Boiling water and steam pressure are the two methods recommended for home canning. In the first step, water that is boiling surrounds the filled jar and its lid.

This technique can be used to preserve a variety of naturally acidic foods, such as tomatoes and other fruits. For low-acid dishes such as vegetables, meats, seafood, and soups, the steam-pressure method must be used. Preparing the food and filling the canisters are essentially identical for both approaches.

The only difference is that a steam-pressure canner can superheat low-acid foods to 240 degrees Fahrenheit, eradicating toxic bacterial spores that can survive boiling at 212 degrees Fahrenheit.

Because fruits and tomatoes are prolific producers and versatile in the kitchen novice canners typically begin with them and the boiling-water method. It is less intricate than the steam-pressure method, and the canner is cheaper. This is the method I will describe here.

The majority of canning equipment is already present in most kitchens. A few inexpensive specialized items are useful: a plastic or stainless steel wide-mouth funnel for filling the jars; a magnetic-tip lid wand for removing lids from hot water; a narrow plastic spatula for removing air bubbles from filled jars; and a jar lifter for safely lifting jars into and out of the canner.

Obviously, you will need home-canning vessels, metal two-piece caps (screw band and lid), and a boiling-water canner. The canner consists of a large, porcelain-coated steel or aluminum container with a tight-fitting lid and a wire rack, preferably made of stainless steel, that fits inside and keeps jars upright, separate, and off the canner's bottom.

When canning, only use ingredients of the highest quality. The majority of fruits and vegetables are at their peak six to twelve hours after harvesting.

Apricots, peaches, pears, and plums should be entirely ripe prior to being canned. However, when creating jam, choose slightly unripe fruits, as they contain the most natural pectin.

Time and work space organization

Canning is not difficult, but it does require a block of time and some organization. Before beginning, you should have your workspace and tools organized.

Begin by cleaning the canisters. Check for nicks and scratches, wash the jars in hot soapy water, clean them thoroughly, and then place them in the canner, filling it with enough water to completely submerge them.

Bring the water to a simmer (180 degrees Fahrenheit), and process the jars for at least ten minutes. Alternately, jars can be heated in the dishwasher using the entire regular cycle; keep the door closed until you're ready to fill them.

In order to aid in the sealing procedure, the metal lids must also be heated. Wash and sterilize the lids, then bring water to a simmer in a small saucepan, turn off the heat, and submerge the lids for at least 10 minutes.

You should not simmer the lids, as this could damage the gasket material. Screw bands can be reused as long as they are not oxidized or damaged, but the closures can only be used once. It is unnecessary to heat the fastener bands.

Prepare your recipe while the canisters are being heated. Hot packs and raw packs are the two methods for filling canisters. Filling heated jars with hot, cooked food is the method of hot-packing.

Using the raw-pack method, uncooked food is packed tightly into heated jars and then covered with boiling syrup, juice, or water. Because hot-packed foods retain more color and flavor, this is the preferred packaging method. Only melons and certain fruits are occasionally raw-packed.

Adhere to the formula.

Follow kitchen-tested recipes precisely, regardless of the cooking method you choose. Do not decrease the quantity of vinegar in pickled items, and do not double jam recipes.

Ascorbic acid or citric acid can be used to prevent discoloration in apples, apricots, peaches, and other light-colored fruits. Use ascorbic acid powder or dissolve 3,000 milligrams of vitamin C tablets in 1 liter of water.

To fill the jars, remove the wire rack of jars from the water and secure it to the rim of the canner. Remove one jar from the canner using a jar lifter, gingerly pour out the hot water, and set the jar on a towel to prevent slipping. Ladle food into the jar while leaving the specified quantity of headspace, or space between the food and the lid. This space enables food to expand during processing and creates a vacuum as the jar cools. Typically, the headspace for preserves, jellies, pickles, and relishes is 14 inches, and for fruits and tomatoes, it is 12 inches.

To eradicate air bubbles, press a spatula against the jar's sides and into the container, using a clean, damp cloth, wipe the top and threads of the container. Place a screw band over a hot lid that has been centered on the container. While holding the lid down with one hand, tighten the band until it becomes resistant.

Once all the canisters have been filled, place them back in the canner. Add additional boiling water until it reaches at least 1 inch above the vessels. The addition of 12 cups of vinegar to the processing water prevents mineral deposits from forming on the vessels.

Increase the heat while the canner is covered. When the water is rapidly boiling, reduce the heat to sustain a gentle boil and set the timer for the number of minutes specified in the recipe. Processing time is proportional to the capacity of the jar and increases as altitude increases. Consult the instructions or contact your local extension office.

Verify the tamper.

When the recommended processing time for the jars has passed, turn off the heat, remove the jars using the jar lifter, and set them on a towel with at least 1 inch of space between each jar to cool. The fastener bands must not be tightened. After 12 to 24 hours, you can ensure that the canisters have sealed properly by examining them.

Each covering should be concave and immovable when pressed in the middle. Remove the screw bands and attempt to remove the lids by lifting them gently. Refrigerate the container and use its contents within a few days if the seal has been broken.

Definition and Purpose of Canning

Canning is a method for preserving food in vessels at high temperatures for an extended period of time, which kills microorganisms and inactivates enzymes that cause food to spoil. As the food cools, the process of heating forces air out of the jar and creates a vacuum seal.

Stock the shelves of your pantry with home-canned preserves, relishes, and condiments so that you can enjoy farmers' market produce throughout the year. While some see canning as a means to preserve their bountiful homegrown harvest, you can also use this tradition of food preservation for small-batch canning to capture the season's finest flavors.

How does Canning Operate

Essentially, when you heat filled, sealed jars, the foods expand and release vapor, forcing the air out of the jars. As it cools, it creates a vacuum seal on the container. The sugar content and acidity can affect canning and shelf life, so it's best to follow a canning recipe when you're just getting started to determine which method is best for the food you'll be canning.

Two Methods of Home Canning

Water-bath Preserving: This method is a low-temperature canning process that is optimal for acidic foods and recipes that contain the appropriate amount of acid. It is suggested for use with fruits, preserves, jellies, salsa, tomatoes, pickles, chutneys, sauces, pie fillings, and condiments.

Pressurized Preserving: Low-acid foods must be preserved using this method at elevated temperatures. It is recommended for meats, vegetables, chiles, and seafood. The USDA advises against using a pressure cooker for canning because there are too many different models that produce variable results.

What do you need at home to preserve

1. Jar lifter tongs: Tongs are used to safely remove processed vessels from hot water and remove them from the processing area.

2. Ladle: A ladle is used to place food in canning vessels.

3. Wide-mouth funnel: A wide-mouth funnel has a broader opening in order to accommodate jars. It makes filling jars easier and preserves the cleanliness of the borders.

4. Jars and seals: Use glass Mason jars with sealed closures for canning. We recommend Ball Mason jugs.

5. Large pot or water-bath canner: If fruits, preserves, jellies, pickles, and salsa are your primary focus, a large pot or water-bath canner will work well.

What can you Can

- Fruits
- Tomatoes
- Vegetables
- Meat, poultry, and fish
- Pellies and jams
- Pickles and fermented vegetables

How to Maximize the Benefits of Homemade Canning

1. Use fresh produce. Produce that is bruised or overripe should be avoided, as should produce that is in prime condition.

2. A water reservoir or pressurized canner? A simmering water bath can be used to preserve acidic foods like pickles, jams, and tomatoes. But non-acidic foods such as broth stocks, unpickled vegetables, and meat must be canned using a pressure canner, a specialized piece of equipment.

3. Fill the vessels while they are still warm. Leave space at the top of each container for closure when placing hot food. After filling it, return it to the simmering water.

4. Listen for popping noises. Once the jar has been correctly sealed, you should hear a pop, and the lid should no longer rise.

5. Overfilling vessels. A decent recipe will instruct you to leave headspace between the food and the rim of the jar. The canning lids will not secure adequately if jars are overfilled. Unsealed jars are not fatal; you can transfer them to the refrigerator and use them within a few days, or reprocess them with enough head space to seal.

How Long Do Canned Goods Remain Safe to Consume?

When stored in a cold, dry location, unopened home-canned foods have a shelf life of one year. Expect a shelf life of approximately two years for homemade preserves made with sugar and processed in a boiling water bath. For food safety, follow canning recipes.

How Can You Tell if Canned Goods Are Spoiled

While the vast majority of canned goods are shelf-stable, these signs indicate that the product inside the can has gone bad:

- The presence of oxygen indicates a breached seal. Also indicative of spoilage is a bulging cover.
- A cover that exhibits oxidation or corrosion
- When the can is opened, it bubbles.
- Moldy or opaque food is unfit for consumption.
- When the container is opened, the food emits an unpleasant smell.

Importance of Ball Canning

It is that time of year again when we break out the pressure canners and get to work. Our weekends are spent in the kitchen for countless hours preserving our homegrown produce. The vast majority of us have been performing the same tune and dance for eons.

Like myself, others may be novices at preserving. Because fresh foods contain a high proportion of water, they are perishable. Canned food is preserved by removing oxygen, destroying enzymes, and preventing the development of bacteria, yeasts, and mold.

Keeping your family safe when consuming home-canned foods is dependent on the use of appropriate canning techniques, Ineffective preservation techniques may result in the production of botulism-causing C. botulinum. In severe instances, botulism can result in death due to facial paralysis, drooling, and drooping eyelids. It is essential to adhere to the following preservation best practices:

- Meticulously select and cleanse fresh produce
- Peel according to the formula,
- Reheating a variety of dishes
- Some dishes are prepared by adding

acids (lemon juice or vinegar).
- Utilizing suitable canisters and self-sealing caps
- Processing vessels in a boiling-water or pressure canner for the required time period.

Acquire a guide to the scientific preservation of food. The Ball Blue Book, the USDA Complete Guide to Domestic Canning, and the University of Georgia Cooperative Extension's "So Easy to preserve" are three highly regarded resources for domestic food preservation.

The recipes contained in these guides have been evaluated for safety and quality. Prior to your initial attempt at preservation, you should read your new book after obtaining it. By doing so, the majority of your concerns will be answered, and you will be able to determine what equipment you need to purchase before beginning.

Benefits of Ball Canning

Until the advent of modern grocery stores, canning was nearly universal in households. It was a necessity and a means of survival. Compare this to modern times. After only a couple of generations, the overwhelming majority of people have lost the ability to preserve food. However, interest in food preservation has increased in recent years, and canning in particular has experienced a surge in popularity. Many factors contribute to this result:

1. Food can be an expensive commodity. Buying or harvesting in-season produce and preserving it in jars can save you money. This is particularly true when you consider the quality of the foods you are receiving. You might be astonished by how gourmet home-canned foods can taste.

2. Preserve the harvest; cultivators will comprehend this concept. You patiently wait a few months for your garden to begin producing, and then you are flooded with far more produce than you are able to handle. Sure, you can give some to your family, friends, and acquaintances, but you'll still have plenty. Canning the surplus fruits and vegetables is a sensible method to prevent waste and enjoy the harvest throughout the year.

3. Many people are concerned about the state of the economy in the current era. People want to be prepared in the event that something occurs to our economy or our ability to affordably buy food. Canning is one of the measures that most people take; if you ask us, it is far more practical than constructing a bomb shelter.

4. Canning your own food is a fantastic way to reduce your environmental footprint. Especially if the food is locally grown, you eliminate the innumerable miles food travels between the farm, the factory, the distributor, and the local store. Additionally, you reduce

packaging pollution because canning jars are reusable and will last for years (excluding lids).

5. Many people appreciate canning because it evokes memories of a simpler era or is a token of appreciation. Perhaps their mother or grandmother participated in the activity. Moreover, preserved foods make wonderful presents. The labor and attention that went into making handmade jam or pickles are far more valuable than the food itself.

6. Homemade cuisine simply tastes better; this is a proven fact. Fresh, locally grown ingredients used to create a high-quality home-canned product cannot be beaten. You could easily pay twice as much for this item in the store. Even if your initial investment does not result in savings (due to purchasing canisters, a canner, etc.), you will have a healthier, tastier product in your pantry. You can also experiment with new flavor combinations and customize recipes to your exact preferences.

7. Health: While canning is not the healthiest method of food preservation (e.g., freezing preserves more nutrients than canning), it does offer a number of advantages. You will know exactly what you are consuming because you canned it yourself. There is no doubt that the cuisine was both fresh and of high quality. In addition, you will consume food that is devoid of additives and preservatives.

In subsequent articles, we will gain a deeper understanding of canning and address common queries and concerns. Included will be the nutrition of canned foods, safety concerns, a discussion of the necessary apparatus, and a comprehensive explanation of both water bath and pressure canning.

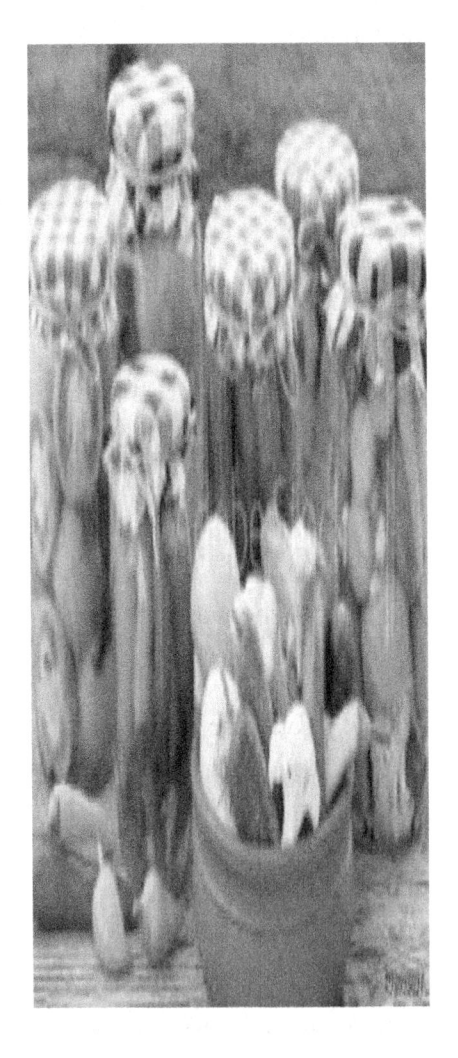

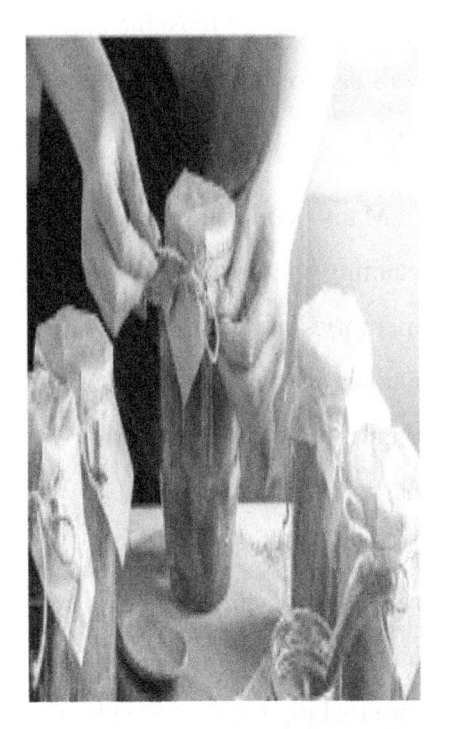

CHAPTER 2

Understanding Canning Basics

During the dead of winter, if you appreciate eating seasonal foods, meals can become quite monotonous. On a blustery day, wouldn't it be pleasant to grab a jar of summer-perfect peaches from your pantry? Canning allows for the preservation of food in hermetic, room-temperature-stable containers.

What to Can

Consider your preferred seasonal cuisines when deciding what to can. Do you favor sun-kissed tomatoes or plump strawberries in the summer? Observe what is plentiful and inexpensive. When plums are piled high on the tables of a farmer's market, it's likely that you will find a decent deal. Not prepared to can maize when it reaches maturity? "You can freeze it and preserve it later," explains Vinton.

Canning is not, however, limited to summer produce. Vinton makes hot pepper jelly in the autumn, citrus curd and marmalade in the winter, and pickled asparagus in the spring.

Canning Methods

There are two domestic canning methods: the boiling water method and the pressure-canning method. Both canning techniques operate in a similar manner. The ingredients are prepared and placed in canisters with special lids that allow for the escape of steam. When the canisters are heated, the food contracts as it cools, creating an airtight seal that can preserve the contents for up to a year.

Low-acid foods, such as most vegetables and proteins, are suitable for pressure canning. To prevent the growth of microbes, these must be heated at a higher temperature in a specialized pressure-Canning device. For significant quantities, we suggest the Presto 23-Quart Pressure Canner, which is also an excellent large-capacity pressure cooker.

Vinton explains that the boiling-water canning procedure is a simple way to get started because it requires minimal equipment. It is appropriate for acidic foods, such as fruit preserves and jellies, salsas, tomatoes, and vegetables made more acidic by the addition of vinegar, lemon juice, or citric acid.

Recipe Selection for Canning

Find a recipe from a reliable, up-to-date source once you've determined what you wish to can. Although it may be alluring to use your great-aunt's yellowing jam recipe, safe canning guidelines have evolved substantially over time.

Follow canning recipes precisely for the best (and most secure) outcomes. A minor adjustment could alter the acidity and encourage the growth of microbes. Vinton states, "However, a chemistry degree is not required for canning." Everything will be successful if you adhere to a modern canning recipe and maintain a tidy kitchen.

Safety Guidelines and Precautions

1. When canning food at home, always use a canner.

2. Low-acid foods must be processed in a pressure canner.

3. Certain foods should never be preserved.

4. Canning requires Masonic vessels.

5. When canning, always use fresh covers.

6. Follow a tried-and-true recipe at all times.

Equipment and Tools for Ball Canning

Canning is a wonderful activity.

There is something special about a fresh jar of homemade jam in the winter: toasting some fresh bread, savoring a hot beverage, and heading out the door to face the day. Or how about a crunchy pickle made from the excess cucumbers and green beans you grew during the summer? Occasionally, a nibble is the only thing that gets you through the day.

With the proper knowledge and apparatus for canning, you can enjoy the flavors of any season year-round.

What tools do you have? What am I lacking

Fruit and vegetable canning is a skill well worth acquiring. What are the necessary instruments to begin?

We have compiled a list of our preferred home canning supplies specifically for you. Also included are a few extras for good measure. Happy preserving!

1. CANNING JARS AND LIDS

There are numerous sizes and shapes of canning vessels. Choose canning vessels that are appropriate for the food being preserved. Choose economical, functional, and well-made canning jars if you intend to store your canned products in your own pantry.

Choose decorative canning vessels if you intend to give away some of the canned goods. We carry canning vessels made by Weck, Quattro Stagione, Le Parfait, Ball, Kerr, and a few others.

Some canning vessels have a single-piece lid, whereas others have a two-piece lid/band combination. There are also canning lids that are reusable and can be used repeatedly. Ensure that you are using the correct-sized lid for your canning jar.

2. CANNING UTILITIES/INSTALLATIONS

The must-have instruments for your canning arsenal, in our opinion, are...

- A pickling funnel of plastic or stainless steel
- A stainless steel ladle
- Rubberized grips on a canning container lifter.
- A reliable set of culinary tongs
- Magnetic lid raiser and froth eliminater

Many of these items are available in packages containing canning implements! View our complete collection of home preservation equipment.

3. A COOKER OR CONSERVATOR

With the addition of a canning rack, canning can be performed in any large pot, but we prefer to use a canner designed for domestic use. Canners come in various sizes, with or without canning racks. Some canners even come as kits with all of the necessary canning equipment.

Because they are reasonably priced, water bath canners are

ideal for beginners. Pressure canners are ideally suited for sophisticated canning techniques, and they can also be used as pressure cookers.

4. GOOD KITCHEN TOWELS

Towels are a necessity for the majority of kitchen projects, but particularly for canning! Use a clean kitchen towel to place hot jars on the counter while they settle, and use a clean kitchen towel to wipe the rim of your jars before sealing.

5. A DECENT BOOK ON HOME CANNING

For processing times and recipes, cookbooks are an excellent resource for fast reference. Select a book on canning that contains recipes for the categories of foods you wish to preserve and detailed instructions on canning techniques.

6. A FOOD MILL OR FOOD SEPARATOR

Food strainers and food mills are a fast and convenient way to grind or puree foods for canning. These items are not required for canning; they are merely a beneficial bonus. Particularly when preparing homemade apple sauce. Blenders and food Processors can perform the same function, but these electrical appliances are required.

Preparing Jars and Lids

INSPECTING YOUR PRESERVATION JARS:

Initially, inspect your jars for flaws, nicks, fractures, unevenness, etc. This is a crucial stage; any defects in your canning jars may result in a failed canning process.

WASHING YOUR CANNING JARS:

If there are no defects, wash your jars with hot, soapy water and a thorough rinsing, or put them through the dishwasher. Do not use anything abrasive on your glass vessels, as this may cause damage.

HEATING YOUR CANNING JARS:

Before filling your jars, you must heat them for 10 minutes to prevent breakage during processing. Fill a saucepan with enough water to cover the jars' lids. On the stove, bring the water to a simmer (180 degrees), and keep the jars in the simmering water until they are ready to be used. Remove the jars from the simmering water as you are ready to fill them, one by one.

Are you new to canning? You may also be interested in Getting Ready to Can.

LIDS AND BANDS:

Choose lids and bands of the appropriate size for the vessels you will be using. Examine them for flaws and damage.

Important: Use only new covers whenever possible, as the rings are reusable.

Wash lids and bands with hot detergent water, followed by hot water rinsing, lacking in bands. Set the containers to be heated aside.

Prior to use, the covers must be heated for 10 minutes. This ensures that the lids seal correctly. Fill a sauce pan with enough water to cover the lids. Heat water to 180 degrees (do not boil). Keep the covers warm until it is time to use them.

Canning Methods and Techniques

First, you must decide which food or product you will eat. Then, keep in mind that low acid requires a pressure canner, whereas high acid requires water immersion. (More on this in a moment.)

It is essential to consider the following factors when selecting food:

1. Choose local fruits and vegetables when possible. If you live near an orchard or pick-your-own farm, you should purchase your produce directly from the farmer. Not only is the product of higher quality, but it also benefits the community. Prior to your visit, please contact us to determine what is available.

2. Consider your landscape. Have you planted strawberries? Try making strawberry jam.

3. What foods does your family consume frequently? Your

family consumes a great deal of peanut butter and jelly sandwiches, right? Make your own homemade grape marmalade.

4. Start with something simple, something you're eager to consume and share. When you open a container containing something you've preserved, you'll feel uplifted. You'll be able to say, "I did that!" It will inspire you to continue advancing.

CHAPTER 3

Water Bath Canning

Water bath canning is a preservation method used to can high-acid foods such as fruits, jams, jellies, pickles, and some tomato products. It is a simple and popular method for home canning that involves processing the filled jars in a large pot of boiling water.

Also, Water bath processing is a processing method used in home canning for high acid foods. Jars are filled with food, sealed loosely with a lid, then boiled completely covered in vigorously boiling water for a prescribed amount of time indicated by the tested recipe you are using.

High-acid foods are items such as jams, jellies, most fruits, pickles, relishes, chutneys, salsas, and tomato products with added acid.

Step-by-Step Guide to Water Bath Canning

Water bath canning is a popular method used to preserve high-acid foods like fruits, pickles, and jams. It involves heating filled jars in boiling water to create a seal and prevent spoilage. Here's a step-by-step guide to water bath canning:

Method 1

1. Gather the necessary equipment: You'll need canning jars with lids and bands, a large pot with a rack or a dedicated water bath canner, a jar lifter, a canning funnel, a bubble remover or plastic spatula, a clean towel, a ladle, and a timer.

2. Prepare your recipe: Choose a tested recipe from a reliable source that is specifically designed for water bath canning. Follow the recipe instructions for preparing the food you plan to can.

3. Sterilize the jars: Wash the jars, lids, and bands in hot, soapy water. Rinse them well and place them in a large pot filled with water. Bring the water to a simmer and let the jars simmer for 10 minutes.

Keep them in the hot water until you're ready to fill them.

4. Prepare the canning bath: Fill your canning pot or large pot with enough water to cover the jars with at least 1 to 2 inches of water. Place the rack at the bottom of the pot to prevent the jars from touching the direct heat.

5. Preheat the water bath: Begin heating the water bath while you're preparing your recipe. Bring the water to a simmer, but not a rolling boil, as you want to avoid splashing hot water when you place the jars.

6. Fill the jars: Using a canning funnel, carefully ladle the hot prepared food into the sterilized jars, leaving the recommended headspace (usually ¼ to ½ inch) at the top. Remove any air bubbles by running a bubble remover or plastic spatula around the inside edges of the jar. Wipe the rim of the jar with a clean towel to remove any spills or food particles.

7. Apply lids and bands: Place a lid on top of each jar, ensuring that the sealing compound is in contact with the rim. Screw the bands onto the jars until they are fingertip-tight—tightened just enough to hold the lid in place but still allow air to escape during processing.

8. Process the jars: Using a jar lifter, carefully lower the filled jars into the preheated water bath, making sure they are fully submerged. If necessary, add more boiling water to the pot to ensure the jars are covered by at least 1 to 2 inches of water. Cover the pot with a lid.

9. Bring the water bath to a boil: Increase the heat and bring the water to a rolling boil. Start the processing time indicated in your recipe only when the water reaches a full boil. Maintain a steady boil throughout the processing time.

10. Process for the recommended time: Follow the recipe's recommended processing time. This time varies depending on the recipe and the altitude of your location. Adjust the processing time if necessary for your altitude.

11. Remove the jars: After the processing time is complete, turn off the heat and carefully remove the jars from the water bath using a jar lifter. Place them on a clean towel or a cooling rack, leaving space between the jars. Avoid tilting or shaking the jars, as this may interfere with the sealing process.

12. Cool and check for seals: Let the jars cool undisturbed for 12 to 24 hours. During this time, you may hear a popping sound, indicating that the lids are sealing. After cooling, press down on the center of each lid to check for a proper seal. If the lid is firm and doesn't move, the jar is sealed. If any jars haven't sealed, you can either reprocess them using a new lid or refrigerate and consume the contents within a few days.

13. Label and store the jars: Once the jars have cooled and you've confirmed that they are properly sealed, label each jar with the contents and the date of canning. Store the jars in a cool, dark place, such as a pantry or cellar, where they can be kept for up to a year.

14. Clean up: Dispose of any unused or spoiled food properly. Wash the canning equipment, including the pot, jar lifter, funnel, and other utensils, in hot, soapy water. Dry and store them in a clean and dry place until your next canning project.

It's important to note that water bath canning is suitable for preserving high-acid foods only. Low-acid foods, such as vegetables, meats, and soups, require pressure canning to ensure safe preservation. Always follow tested recipes and guidelines from reliable sources to ensure proper food safety practices.

Additionally, altitude can affect the processing time needed for water bath canning. If you live at an elevation above 1,000 feet (305 meters), you may need to adjust the processing time to compensate for the lower boiling point of water. Consult a trusted source for altitude adjustments specific to your location.

Method 2

1. Place the food in the canisters.

2. Replace the caps.

3. Place something on the bottom of the vessel between the jars and the pot's bottom.

4. Place the bottles upright in the water. Make certain that the vessels are submerged in 3 to 5 cm (1 to 2 inches) of water. Adding more water if necessary. (Resist the temptation to deceive by placing the jars on their sides; if

you do, the jars may release their contents instead of air!)

5. Cover the saucepan.

6. Only when the water reaches a roiling boil do you begin timing. If it was already boiling before the vessels were added, this refers to when the water returns to a rolling boil. Not included in the processing time is the time required to heat the water in the canner. (You'll have to frequently lift the lid to determine when the water has reached a complete boil.)

7. Allow the canner to simmer for the required duration. During this interval, it is most optimal to have the canner's lid on.

8. When the time is up, turn off the heat and remove the lid from the canner. (Leave the canner where it is, or move it if you can do so safely and need the burner.)

9. Leave the vessels in the canner in their current position.

10. Program a five-minute timer;

11. After 5 minutes, remove the jars from the oven and place them on a towel or a wire rack in a location that is protected from chilly drafts.

12. Do not cover jars; do not touch rings (unless using Tattler lids); do not tilt or invert jars; nor attempt to sanitize or dry them at this time. Any moisture present will rapidly evaporate.

13. 12 to 24 hours should pass without touching the canisters.

14. Remove the screw bands and verify the flat lid's correct seal.

15. Put items that did not seal in the refrigerator and regard them as opened.

16. Wipe down the jars, label and date the jars, and store them in a cold, dark place without the screw bands.

If you follow any of the methods outlined above, your water-bathed food products will be 100% safe and of superior, long-lasting quality. The procedure is based on scientific research and incorporates a large amount of error margin to account for the variables of everyday life.

Preparing the Recipe

Here's a step-by-step guide on how to prepare the water bath canning recipes

1. Strawberry Jam:

Ingredients:

- Fresh
- strawberries, sugar
- Lemon juice.

Instructions:

• Sterilize jars and lids: Wash jars and lids in hot, soapy water and rinse well. Place them in a large pot and cover with water. Bring the water to a simmer and let the jars and lids sit in hot water until ready to use.

• Prepare the strawberries: Wash and hull the strawberries. Crush them using a potato masher or pulse them in a food processor, depending on the desired texture.

- Cook the jam: In a large pot, combine the crushed strawberries, sugar, and lemon juice. Stir well. Place the pot over medium-high heat and bring the mixture to a boil, stirring frequently. Reduce the heat to low and simmer for about 20-25 minutes or until the jam thickens.

- Fill and process the jars: Remove the sterilized jars from the hot water bath and place them on a clean towel. Ladle the hot jam into the jars, leaving a ¼-inch headspace. Use a clean, non-metallic utensil to remove air bubbles. Wipe the rims of the jars with a clean, damp cloth. Apply the lids and screw on the bands fingertip tight.

- Process in a water bath: Place the filled jars in a water bath canner, ensuring they are covered with at least 1 inch of water. Bring the water to a gentle boil and process for 10 minutes. Adjust processing time for altitude if necessary. After processing, carefully remove the jars from the canner and let them cool undisturbed for 12-24 hours. Check the seals before storing.

2. Salsa Verde:

Ingredients:

- Tomatillos
- onions
- jalapeno peppers
- garlic
- cilantro
- lime juice
- Salt.

Instructions:

- Sterilize jars and lids: Follow the same sterilization process mentioned in the previous recipe.

- Prepare the ingredients: Remove the husks from the tomatillos and rinse them well. Peel and roughly chop the onions and jalapeno peppers. Peel the garlic cloves. Rinse and chop the cilantro.

- Blend the ingredients: In a blender or food processor, combine the tomatillos, onions, jalapeno peppers, garlic, cilantro, lime juice, and salt. Blend until smooth.

- Cook the salsa: Pour the blended salsa into a large pot. Bring it to a boil over medium-high heat, then reduce the heat and simmer for about 10 minutes, stirring occasionally.

- Fill and process the jars: Remove the sterilized jars from the hot water bath and place them on a clean towel. Ladle the hot salsa into the jars, leaving a ½-inch headspace. Remove air bubbles and wipe the rims. Apply the lids and screw on the bands fingertip tight.

• Process in a water bath: Place the filled jars in a water bath canner, ensuring they are covered with at least 1 inch of water. Bring the water to a gentle boil and process for 15 minutes. Adjust processing time for altitude if necessary. Remove the jars from the canner and let them cool undisturbed for 12-24 hours. Check the seals before storing.

3. Peach Slices:

Ingredients:

- Fresh peaches
- water
- sugar
- Lemon juice.

Instructions:

• Sterilize jars and lids: Follow the same sterilization process mentioned earlier.

• Prepare the peaches: Bring a large pot of water to a boil. Meanwhile, prepare an ice bath in a bowl or sink. Score a small "X" on the bottom of each peach. Immerse the peaches in boiling water for about 30 seconds, then transfer them to the ice bath. Peel the skin off the peaches. Cut the peaches in half, remove the pits, and slice them.

- Prepare the syrup: In a large pot, combine water, sugar, and lemon juice. Heat the mixture over medium

- Cook the peaches: Add the peach slices to the pot with the syrup. Bring the mixture to a boil over medium-high heat, then reduce the heat and simmer for about 5 minutes, or until the peaches are slightly tender.

- Fill and process the jars: Remove the sterilized jars from the hot water bath and place them on a clean towel. Pack the hot peach slices into the jars, leaving a ½-inch headspace. Ladle the hot syrup over the peaches, ensuring they are fully covered. Remove air bubbles and wipe the rims. Apply the lids and screw on the bands fingertip tight.

- Process in a water bath: Place the filled jars in a water bath canner, ensuring they are covered with at least 1 inch of water. Bring the water to a gentle boil and process for 20 minutes. Adjust processing time for altitude if necessary. Remove the jars from the canner and let them cool undisturbed for 12-24 hours. Check the seals before storing.

4. Bread and Butter Pickles:

Ingredients:

- Cucumbers
- onions
- white vinegar,
- sugar
- mustard seeds
- celery seeds
- turmeric
- Salt.

Instructions:

- Sterilize jars and lids. Slice cucumbers and onions. In a large pot, combine vinegar, sugar, mustard seeds, celery seeds, turmeric, and salt. Bring to a boil, stirring until the sugar dissolves. Add cucumber and onion slices and cook for 5 minutes. Pack hot pickles into jars, leaving a ½-inch headspace. Wipe rims, apply lids and bands, and process in a water bath for 10 minutes.

5. Blueberry Preserves:

Ingredients:

- Fresh blueberries
- sugar
- Lemon juice.

Instructions:

• Sterilize jars and lids. In a large pot, combine blueberries, sugar, and lemon juice. Bring to a boil, stirring frequently. Reduce heat and simmer until thickened. Ladle hot preserves into jars, leaving a ¼-inch headspace. Wipe rims, apply lids and bands, and process in a water bath for 15 minutes.

Remember to always follow proper canning procedures, including sterilizing jars and lids, maintaining the correct headspace, and processing jars for the recommended time in the water bath.

Preparing Jars and Lids

Preparing jars and lids for canning or preserving food is an important step to ensure the safety and longevity of your preserved goods. Here's a general guide on how to prepare jars and lids for canning:

1. Gather the necessary supplies:

- Jars: Choose canning jars specifically designed for preserving foods. They should be free of cracks, chips, or defects.

- Lids: Use new, unused canning lids with a rubber seal. Avoid reusing old lids, as they may not provide a proper seal.

- Bands: Metal bands or rings are used to secure the lids on the jars during processing. They can be reused as long as they are in good condition.

2. Inspect the jars:

Examine each jar for any signs of damage, such as cracks or chips. Discard any defective jars as they may not seal properly.

3. Wash the jars:

Thoroughly clean the jars with hot, soapy water. Use a bottle brush to reach the bottom of the jars. Rinse well to remove any soap residue.

4. Sterilize the jars:

There are several methods to sterilize jars:

- Oven method: Place the jars on a baking sheet and heat them in a preheated oven at 275°F (135°C) for 20 minutes. Keep them in the oven until ready to use.

- Boiling water bath method: Submerge the jars in a large pot of boiling water. Ensure they are fully covered with water and boil for 10 minutes. Keep them in the hot water until ready to use.

- Dishwasher method: Place the jars in a dishwasher and run a hot water cycle. Keep them in the dishwasher until ready to use.

5. Prepare the lids:

Check the lids for any dents or defects. Place them in a small pot of hot, but not boiling, water. Keep them simmering over low heat until ready to use. Do not boil the lids, as excessive heat can compromise the seal.

6. Fill the jars:

Once your recipe is ready, carefully remove a sterilized jar from the oven, boiling water bath, or dishwasher. Fill the jar with your prepared food, leaving the recommended headspace (the space between the top of the food and the rim of the jar) specified in your canning recipe.

7. Wipe the jar rims:

Using a clean, damp cloth or paper towel, wipe the rims of the jars to remove any food residue or moisture. A clean rim ensures a proper seal.

8. Apply the lids and bands:

Using a magnetic lid lifter or clean tongs, remove a lid from the hot water and place it on the jar's rim. Then, secure the lid in place with a band, tightening it until it is just fingertip tight. Do not overtighten.

9. Process the jars:

Follow the recommended processing method and time specified in your canning recipe. This may involve using a boiling water bath or a pressure canner. The processing time will vary depending on the food being preserved and the altitude of your location.

10. Remove and cool the jars:

Once the processing time is complete, carefully remove the jars from the canner using jar lifters. Place them on a clean towel or a cooling rack, leaving some space between them to allow for air circulation. Let the jars cool undisturbed for 12 to 24 hours.

11. Check the seal:

After the jars have cooled, check the seals by pressing down on the center of each lid. If the lid is firm and doesn't flex or pop, it is properly sealed. If a jar did not seal, refrigerate it immediately and consume its contents within a few days.

Properly preparing jars and lids is essential for successful home canning.

Filling Jars and Removing Air Bubbles

Filling jars properly and removing air bubbles is an essential step in preserving food and ensuring its long shelf life. Whether you're canning fruits, vegetables, jams, or pickles, following the correct procedures will help maintain food quality and prevent spoilage. This guide will take you through the step-by-step process of filling jars and removing air bubbles for effective preservation.

Materials Needed:

1. **Jars:** Ensure you have clean, sterilized jars specifically designed for canning. Choose the appropriate size and type of jar for the food you are preserving.

2. **Canning lids and bands:** Use new lids for each canning session to ensure a proper seal.

3. **Canning funnel:** This helps to pour liquids into jars without spilling.

4. **Bubble remover or spatula:** A long, non-metallic utensil used to remove air bubbles from filled jars.

5. **Clean cloth or paper towel:** To wipe jar rims and ensure a clean seal.

Step 1: Prepare Your Jars and Equipment

Before starting the filling process, gather all your

materials and ensure they are clean and in good condition. Wash the jars, lids, and bands in hot, soapy water, rinse them thoroughly, and place them in a pot of boiling water for 10 minutes to sterilize. Keep the jars warm until you're ready to fill them.

Step 2: Prepare Your Recipe and Fill the Jars

Follow your recipe for preparing the food you wish to preserve. Once the food is ready, use a canning funnel to fill the jars, leaving the recommended headspace indicated in your recipe (usually around 1/4 to 1/2 inch from the top). Be careful not to overfill, as it can interfere with the sealing process.

Step 3: Remove Air Bubbles

After filling each jar, use a bubble remover or spatula to gently release any trapped air bubbles. Insert the tool along the inside edge of the jar, moving it up and down to release the air. Repeat this process around the entire circumference of the jar to ensure thorough removal of air bubbles. This step is crucial, as trapped air can lead to spoilage and compromised sealing.

Step 4: Adjust Headspace

Once air bubbles are removed, check the headspace again and adjust if necessary. Add more food or liquid to maintain the recommended headspace, ensuring it remains consistent across all filled jars.

Step 5: Wipe Jar Rims

Using a clean cloth or paper towel, carefully wipe the rims

of the jars to remove any food particles, liquids, or grease. A clean rim ensures a proper seal between the lid and the jar.

Step 6: Apply Lids and Bands

Retrieve the sterilized lids from the hot water and place them on the jars. Secure each lid in place with a band, screwing it on until it is finger-tight. Avoid overtightening, as this can interfere with the sealing process.

Step 7: Process or Store Jars

Once the jars are properly sealed, they can be processed according to your recipe's instructions, which may involve water bath canning or pressure canning. If the recipe does not require processing, you can simply store the jars in a cool, dark place.

Step 8: Check Seals and Store Properly

After the jars have cooled for 12-24 hours, check the seals by pressing down on the center of each lid. A properly sealed lid should not flex or move. Any unsealed jars should be refrigerated and consumed within a few days. Label the sealed jars with the contents and date before storing them in a cool, dry, and dark location.

By following these steps, you can ensure that your jars are filled correctly, air bubbles are removed, and your preserved food is stored safely.

Here are a few additional tips to consider:

1. Use the right jar sizes: It's important to choose jars that are the appropriate size for your recipe. Overfilled jars can lead to inadequate headspace, which may result in the food expanding during processing and causing the jars to break or not seal properly.

2. Avoid using metal utensils: When removing air bubbles, always use non-metallic tools like bubble removers or spatulas. Metal utensils can scratch the inside of the jars and increase the risk of bacterial contamination.

3. be gentle when releasing air bubbles: While removing air bubbles, be careful not to stir or agitate the contents excessively. Vigorous stirring can introduce more air into the jar, defeating the purpose of removing the bubbles.

4. Ensure a proper seal: A proper seal is crucial for preserving food. After processing or cooling, check the jars for any signs of unsealed lids, such as lids that pop up and down when pressed. Unsealed jars should be refrigerated and consumed promptly.

5. Store jars correctly: Store your sealed jars in a cool, dry, and dark place. Avoid exposure to direct sunlight or extreme temperature fluctuations, as they can compromise the quality and safety of the preserved food.

6. Label and date your jars: Properly labeling your jars with the contents and the date of preservation helps you keep track of the freshness and allows you to consume them in a timely manner. Use waterproof labels or permanent markers to ensure the information stays intact during storage.

Applying Lids and Processing Jars

1. Gather the necessary equipment:

- **Jars:** Select jars specifically designed for canning, such as Mason jars or Ball jars. Ensure they are free from cracks or chips.

- **Lids:** Use new lids for each canning session. Lids have a sealing compound that is only good for one use.

- **Bands:** Bands are the metal rings that secure the lids to the jars. You can reuse bands as long as they are in good condition.

- **Canning pot:** Use a large pot with a rack at the bottom to hold the jars and allow for proper water circulation.

- **Canning tools:** Have a jar lifter, lid lifter, funnel, and a bubble remover handy. These tools make the process easier and safer.

2. Prepare the jars:

- Wash the jars, lids, and bands in hot, soapy water. Rinse them well to remove any soap residue.

    - Inspect the jars for cracks or chips. Discard any damaged jars as they may not seal properly.

- Place the jars in the canning pot and fill it with enough water to cover the jars. Bring the water to a simmer (not boiling) to keep the jars hot.

3. Prepare the lids and bands:

- while the jars are simmering, prepare the lids. Place them in a small saucepan and cover with hot, but not boiling, water. Keep the water warm, but not simmering.

- Avoid boiling the lids, as excessive heat may damage the sealing compound.

4. Fill the jars:

- using a funnel, carefully ladle the prepared food or liquid into the hot jars, leaving the recommended headspace (the space between the food and the rim of the jar). Refer to a trusted canning recipe for the appropriate headspace.

- Remove air bubbles by sliding a bubble remover or a non-metallic utensil around the inside edges of the jar.

5. Apply the lids:

- Remove a lid from the hot water using a lid lifter or tongs. Place it on top of the jar, making sure the sealing compound is facing down.

- Secure the lid with a band, tightening it only until it is finger-tight. Do not overtighten, as air needs to escape during processing.

6. Process the jars:

- once all the jars are filled and lids are applied, use a jar lifter to place the jars onto the rack in the canning pot.

- Ensure the water level in the pot covers the jars by at least one inch. Add more boiling water if necessary.

- bring the water to a rolling boil and start the processing time specified in the canning recipe. Adjust the processing time if you are at a higher altitude.

• Maintain a steady boil throughout the entire processing time.

7. Remove and cool the jars:

• after the processing time is complete, turn off the heat and carefully remove the jars from the canning pot using a jar lifter.

• Place the jars on a towel or a cooling rack, leaving some space between them. Avoid touching the lids or bands.

• Allow the jars to cool undisturbed for 12 to 24 hours. You may hear a popping sound as the lids seal.

8. Check the seals and store the jars:

• once the jars have cooled, press down on the center of each lid to check if it is concave and firmly sealed. If the lid springs back, refrigerate the jar and consume its contents within a few days.

• Remove the bands from the sealed jars and wipe them clean. Store the jars in a cool, dark place, such as a pantry or cellar. Label the jars with the contents and the date of processing for easy identification.

9. Dealing with unsealed jars:

• if you find any jars that did not seal properly, there are a few options:

- **Refrigerate and consume:** Place the unsealed jar in the refrigerator and consume its contents within a few days.

• **Reprocess:** Remove the lid, check the jar rim for any nicks or debris, replace with a new lid, and process again using the same processing time.

• **Freeze:** Transfer the contents of the unsealed jar to a freezer-safe container and freeze it for longer storage.

10. Cleaning and storing equipment:

• Wash the canning pot, jar lifter, lid lifter, funnel, and bubble remover in hot, soapy water. Rinse them thoroughly and allow them to air dry.

• Store the equipment in a clean and dry place until your next canning session.

Remember, it's important to follow trusted canning recipes and guidelines to ensure safe food preservation. Properly processed and sealed jars can provide long-term storage for various foods. Enjoy the satisfaction of homemade preserves, pickles, and other delicious treats throughout the year!

Cooling, Storing, and Checking Seals

Canning is a fantastic way to preserve fresh produce, jams, jellies, and other foods. It allows you to enjoy the flavors of summer all year round. One critical aspect of successful canning is ensuring proper cooling, storing, and checking seals. In this guide, we will walk you through the steps to ensure your canned goods are safe and well-preserved.

1. Cool the Jars:

- after the canning process, remove the jars from the canner and place them on a clean towel or a cooling rack.

- Avoid placing the hot jars on a cold surface as it may cause thermal shock and lead to breakage.

- Allow the jars to cool undisturbed for 12 to 24 hours. This cooling time is essential for the formation of a proper seal.

2. Check the Seals:

- after the jars have cooled, gently press down on the center of each lid. The lid should be concave and should not move or make a popping sound.

- Alternatively, you can use a finger to tap the center of the lid. A sealed lid will produce a solid, dull sound, while an unsealed lid will produce a hollow, tinny sound.

- visually inspect the lids for any signs of leakage or bulging. A properly sealed lid should be flat and firm against the jar.

3. Test the Seals:

- for an additional layer of assurance, you can perform a water bath test on the sealed jars.

- Fill a basin or sink with enough water to cover the jars completely.

- gently place the jars in the water bath and ensure they are fully submerged.

- bring the water to a simmer and maintain it for 10 minutes.

- After 10 minutes, carefully remove the jars from the water bath and place them on a towel to cool.

- Inspect the lids again for any signs of leakage or bulging. A jar that has passed the water bath test is considered to have a reliable seal.

4. Storing Canned Goods:

- once you have confirmed that all the jars have sealed correctly, it's time to store them.

    - Remove any screw bands or rings from the jars. They are not required for storage and can rust or interfere with the seal.

- Clean the jars and lids with a damp cloth to remove any residue.

- Label each jar with its contents and the date of canning. This information will help you keep track of freshness.

- Choose a cool, dark, and dry location for storage, such as a pantry or a cellar. Excessive heat, direct sunlight, and humidity can degrade the quality of the canned goods.

- Arrange the jars in an upright position, leaving some space between them to allow for air circulation.

5. Checking Seals during Storage:

- over time, it's essential to periodically check the seals of your stored canned goods to ensure they remain intact.

- gently press down on the center of each lid, as you did when checking the seals after canning. The lid should remain concave and firmly attached.

- if a lid is loose or pops up and down, the seal has likely failed, and the contents should be discarded.

- Inspect the jars for any signs of spoilage, such as mold growth, off odors, or unusual discoloration. If any of these signs are present, do not consume the contents.

CHAPTER 4

Pressure Canning

Introduction to Pressure Canning

In order to preserve and encapsulate foods in jars, pressure canners use heat, pressure, and a specific amount of time. Meat and vegetables are low-acid ingredients that must be processed in a pressure canner. To destroy all bacteria, pathogens, and toxins they produce, they must be heated to 240°F and held there for the time specified in the recipe.

Due to the pressure, the temperature may exceed the point at which water boils. At 10 pounds of tension, using a weighted-gauge canner, the ambient temperature will reach 240°F (at or below 1,000 feet above sea level), meaning it is hot enough to eliminate the toxin-emitting bacterial spores.

If your location is more than 1,000 feet above sea level, you must increase the process temperature by increasing the pounds of pressure; the processing duration remains the same.

Due to the need to sustain and monitor the pressure level, there are more components in the pressure canner than in the water bath. Each pressure canner is slightly different, so it is advisable to familiarize yourself with the model you possess. Frequently, companies provide an online version of the owner's manual if you do not have it.

In addition to the pot and the lid, the essential components of a pressure canner include a rack to prevent jars from resting directly on the bottom's heat, a gasket or tightening knobs for sealing the lid to the pot, and pressure monitoring apparatus (either a gauge or a weight). If you have a gasket, you should routinely inspect it to ensure that it seals. If the seal is not preserved, the pressure cannot be maintained. Many hardware stores sell new gaskets, and you can also find them online; however, you should have your model number handy, as there are a variety of types.

In addition to the overpressure plug, which is typically included in the same shipment, it is also necessary to replace the plug. If, for whatever reason, your pressure rose too high, this would explode and rapidly release the pressure, (Probably shattering your vessels along the way.) There is a dial or weight on the top of every pressure canner. This is the regulator for pressure. The pressure regulator regulates the internal canner pressure. The pressure gauge or weight is the means by which you monitor the device's internal pressure.

Periodically, its accuracy should be verified. Extension offices at agricultural universities frequently provide this service. The pressure indicator is an additional safety feature that allows you to determine whether or not the instrument contains pressure.

The vent enables steam to escape, thereby creating the

vacuum that helps seal the jars. The pressure regulator is the tiny weight that fits over the exhaust. It maintains pressure until it reaches 15 pounds, at which point it begins to vibrate, releasing pressure.

Food canned under pressure

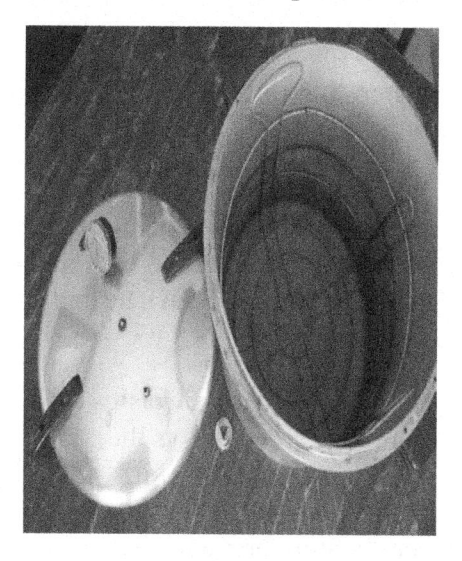

There are three varieties of pressure regulators for canners:

1. One-Piece Pressure Regulator: To adjust the pounds of pressure in this form of pressure canner, add or remove weights. To initiate the pressurization procedure, place the regulator atop the vent pipe. Utilize your stovetop's heat to regulate the gain and loss of heat and pressure within the pressure canner. This type of regulator shakes and jangles as its weight limit approaches.

2. A dial regulator displays the precise pressure within the pressure canner. Utilize your stovetop's heat to regulate the gain and loss of heat and pressure within the pressure canner. Annually, the accuracy of a dial-guage regulator must be examined.

3. Weighted-Guage Regulator: The weighted regulator is a disk-shaped piece of metal that must be placed on top of the exhaust pipe in order to calculate the correct pounds of pressure. As the weight limit approaches, it shakes and rumbles like a single-piece regulator.

If you do not have a jar rack, you may use jar rings to shield the jars from direct heat by placing them on the bottom of the saucepan.

Here is an in-depth guide to using a pressure canner.

See our page on Pressure Canning Principles for information on the "why" behind all these procedures, including the underlying theory and rationale. Understanding why can improve one's proficiency with how.

But let's move on to the actual practice.

1. VERIFY THE NECESSARY PRESSURE.

Check the required pressure before beginning a recipe or set of instructions. Make mental adjustments based on your altitude, as "altitude increases the pressure required for pressure canning."

2. EVALUATE THE REQUIRED PROCESSING TIMES

"Always double- and even triple-check your processing times to ensure that you are using the correct time for your packing method and jar size."

3. CHECK THE WATER NEEDS OF YOUR CANER

It is 3 liters (US quarts) for modern Presto 16- and 23-quart canners. Other brands, models, and sizes will be distinct.

And don't neglect to add a few tablespoons or sprays of vinegar to the water so that your jars and canner remain spotless!

Unlike boiling-water canning, pressure canning does not require vessels to be completely submerged in water.

4. FILL UP THE JARS.

Place the canisters upright. (Resist the temptation to deceive by laying the jars on their sides; if you do, the jars may release their contents instead of air!).

When placing the vessels in the water, the water should not be boiling.

For a heated pack, bring water to a simmer (approximately 80 degrees Celsius or 180 degrees Fahrenheit, if you have a candy thermometer);

Around 60 degrees Celsius (140 degrees Fahrenheit) is the optimal temperature for undercooked fish. This lower temperature prevents the somewhat cooler jars from experiencing a temperature shock.

(Note that the temperature of the water in the pot at this point has nothing to do with food safety; rather, it's about preventing thermal shock, which could cause the jars to fracture.)

5. GO AHEAD AND VENT

Have a nice vent; you deserve it!

1. Lock and load — place the lid on the container and secure it;

2. Leave the weighted gauge off if you have a modern canner. In older canning vessels, leave the petcock open.

3. Increase the heat and bring the water to a simmer in the canner.

4. Be patient, allow the liquid to continue to boil, and wait approximately 10 to 20 minutes, based on the capacity of your canner, until you begin to see steam.

5. Set a timer for 10 minutes once you observe a steady stream of steam emanating from a vent pipe, air vent, or cover lock.

Turn off the heat, remove the lid when it is safe to do so heat-wise while being careful of sudden steam, replace the seal if you have a spare on hand (this is a good reason to), and repeat the entire process, including the 10-minute vent.

NOTE: If you are pressure-canning fish or seafood, the required venting time may be prolonged. Follow the venting instructions outlined in your recipe's testing.

What is high-pressure canning?

In pressure canning (not to be confused with pressure cooking), food is processed at a higher temperature with specialized equipment to prevent spoilage. To preserve "low acid" fruits and vegetables, pressure canning is required. ("High acid" foods such as pickling cucumbers and tomatoes, as well as berries and fruit, are easily preserved by water-bath canning.) In a moment, we'll delve deeper into this topic.

You must invest in a canner (many cost around $100), but the same vessel can be used for both water bath and pressure cooking. It may appear intimidating, but it is comparable to the majority of things. Once you've done it a few times, pressure canning is no more difficult than conventional canning. However, if you've never attempted canning before, we generally advise you to begin with water-bath canning to create jam, pickles, or tomato sauce.

Those who have an abundance of fruits and vegetables from a garden or farmers' market will find pressure canning to be a worthwhile "project." Why attempt to can?

- Perhaps your mother's pressure canner and three shelves of glass canning vessels have been passed down to you. Or, did you inherit or purchase your canning apparatus at a garage sale?
- This year, perhaps you expanded your vegetable garden by twofold. Or did you expand your community-supported agriculture (CSA) membership to include mass purchases?
- Or you're ready to go beyond fast refrigerator jams and pickles to preserve the harvest for an entire year!

Which foods require canning under pressure

The food's acidity (pH) determines how it must be processed for canning. We do not expect you to know your food's pH! However, it all boils down to the amount of acid. A water bath canner can be used to can acidic foods such as berries and pickles with a pH of 4.6 or less. Low-acid foods, such as vegetables and proteins, must be processed in a pressure canner if their pH is greater than 4.62.

Why? Botulism is caused by the hazardous bacteria Clostridium botulinum, which can only be eliminated by preserving "low-acid" foods under pressure. Vegetables with minimal acidity, poultry, meats, seafood, soups, stocks, and stews are all easily preserved. Specifically:

Low-acid vegetables consist of artichokes, asparagus, green beans, lima beans, carrots, maize, mushrooms, okra, onions, peas, potatoes, pumpkin, and winter squash.

Cantaloupe and watermelon are fruits that are mild in acidity. (All other fruits are acidic, including berries, cherries, grapes, nectarines, oranges, peaches, and plums.)

What You Will Enjoy About Pressure Canning

- You can preserve an extensive assortment of native or locally produced vegetables, poultry, meats, and even seafood.
- Produce, meat, and chicken can be purchased at a discount in quantity.
- You can stock your shelves with home-canned convenience foods, such as legumes, lentils, chickpeas, chicken, chilis, soups, broths, and pumpkin or squash for pies.
- During protracted power outages or a malfunctioning freezer, your canned goods will not spoil.
- If cared for properly, modern glass canning jars will last for many years; therefore, by preserving your jars for reuse, you will reduce your waste.
- The freedom to brag There is nothing more impressive than displaying dozens, if not hundreds, of canisters of home-canned treats.

Supplies for Pressure-Canning

What materials are necessary to begin? The instruments of the trade are as follows:

- You need a pressure canner (not a pressure cooker). Depending on quantity and quality, the price of a pressure canner ranges from $100 to $500.
- **Note:** The U.S. Department of Agriculture recommends using caution when canning in electric pressure cookers or traditional pressure

cookers and does not recommend canning in small pressure cookers or using cooking periods intended for pressure canners.

- Canning jars, bands, and covers are required. Jars of the quart size cost approximately $1 each, while a dozen single-use closures cost between $3 and $4. You may reuse canning jars and bands, but not the lids; purchase a fresh bundle.
- It is helpful to have canning accessories, such as a ladle, a canning funnel with a wide mouth, a container lifter, plenty of clean kitchen towels, and potholders. In addition, a digital timer and a magnetic lid lifter are beneficial.
- You need either a conventional range with coil heating elements or a gas range. A smooth-top range may not be practical or secure. Check with your stove's manufacturer to see if it supports simmering water baths or pressure canning.
- Time is needed. Preparation, processing, and cooling of a single canner full of jars (4 to 20 pints) may require three to four hours or longer. For maximum flavor and nutritional value, you must promptly preserve an abundance of fresh vegetables, meat, or poultry that is ready to be processed.
- For preparing the food, setting up the clean, empty jars, and allowing the jars to chill overnight, you will need countertops and cutting boards.
- Your canned foods require shelf space for storage.

How to Prepare Delicious Canned Foods

1. Familiarize yourself with the manual that arrived with your pressure canner. Find the manufacturer's instructions for this model online, or contact the manufacturer for assistance if you do not have them.

2. If your canner has a dial gauge, have it calibrated once a year to ensure accuracy. Check the website of your state's or county's Cooperative Extension or contact your local Extension office to learn where you can get it tested. Or, directly contact the manufacturer of your canner.

3. Plan to use either brand-new or relatively-new Mason jars in sizes appropriate for your product. Old jars with wire bails and glass closures, decorative glass storage jars, and recycled pickle and peanut butter jars can be used for other purposes.

4. Use a dishwasher to clean your jars, but only a stovetop to prepare your canned products. Canning food in a dishwasher, oven, or microwave is utterly unsafe.

5. Do not alter the proportions of ingredients and do not add thickeners or other unspecified ingredients to the proven recipe you are using.

6. Follow the instructions for filling the jars; leave just the right amount of headspace and resist the temptation to overfill in order to get every last bit of product into the jars. The specified head space enables the food to expand without interfering with the lid's seal as the jar cools, resulting in a strong vacuum.

7. Observe the prescribed periods for venting and cooling the canner. Waiting the full time is required to assure both the safety of the finished product and your own safety (e.g., from steam burns).

8. Consume preserved foods within a year for optimal flavor and nutritional value.

9. You should only can foods that you and your family will consume and enjoy, and you will enjoy the experience from the first to the last bite.

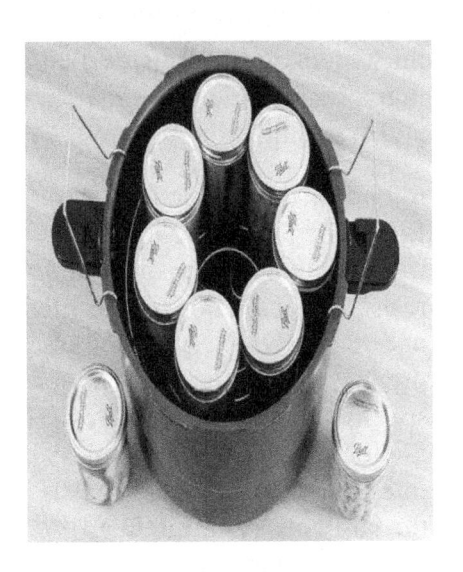

A Step-by-Step Guide to Pressure-Canning:

Before beginning, prepare your low-acid preservation recipe. Here are recipes for safe pressure-preserving!

Method 1

1. Assemble materials. Ensure all canning jars are spotless by washing them in hot, soapy water, rinsing them thoroughly, and letting them air dry. Ensure that all jars, lids, and bands are adequately sized. There should be no chips or cracks on the rim of the container.

2. Pre-heat vessels. Place the jars in a large pot with sufficient hot water to submerge them. Add lid. Bring the water to a simmer for 10 minutes at 180°F.

3. Set up your pressure canner with the rack and 2 to 3 inches of water that has been brought to a simmer and maintained at a simmer until you are ready to fill jars.

4. Today's lids do not need to be heated in simmering water to activate the sealing compound before being placed on jars.

5. Prepare your produce using one of our low-acid, pressure-canning recipes. Using a ladle and funnel, fill each container with the prepared food and liquid that is required.

6. Remove any confined air bubbles by inserting a rubber spatula or plastic canning wand between the jar and food. Leave adequate headspace (1/4", 1/2", or 1" according to recipe instructions).

7. Remove any food residue from the rims of the canisters by wiping them with a clean, damp cloth.

8. Place the lid on each jar, apply the screw band, and

secure by hand. Using the jar lifter, position the jars on the tray within the pressure canner, which contains 2 to 3 inches of simmering water. Do not allow the canisters to come into contact.

9. Lock the canner's lid in position while leaving the vent pipe open. Adjust the heat to medium-high to generate vapor in the vent pipe. Allow steam to escape through the vent pipe for 10 minutes, or until steam creates a steady flow, to ensure that the canner contains no air (only steam). Use the weight or method specified for your canner to seal the vent. Monitor and regulate the temperature to reach the specified pressure.

10. Adjust the pressure and cooking time for altitude (see the altitude chart). Turn the heat off. Leave the canner alone (do not remove the weighted gauge) until the pressure reaches zero. Ten minutes later, remove the weight and release the lid while tilting it away from you. Allow the canisters to cool for 10 minutes more.

11. using a jar lifter, remove the jars from the pressure canner and place them upright on a towel. Leave the vessels alone for 12 to 24 hours.

12. Remove the screw bands and inspect the seals on the lids. Each covering should not bend when the center is gently pressed. If the lid flexes, try gingerly lifting it by the rim with your fingernail. Lids that are properly sealed will remain attached. If the lid fails to seal within 24 hours, refrigerate the product immediately.

Method 2

Step 1: Gather the necessary equipment

- Pressure canner: Ensure you have a reliable pressure canner with a tight-fitting lid, a pressure gauge, and a vent or petcock.
- Canning jars: Use jars specifically designed for canning, such as Mason jars, along with new lids and bands.
- Canning utensils: Have a jar lifter, a lid lifter, a canning funnel, a bubble remover, and a non-metallic spatula or chopstick.

Step 2: Prepare the canning area

- Choose a clean, well-lit, and well-ventilated area for canning.
- Clean and sanitize your work surface, equipment, and jars thoroughly.

Step 3: Prepare the food

- Select fresh, high-quality ingredients for canning.
- Follow a trusted recipe for the specific food you're canning.
- Prepare the food as instructed by the recipe, ensuring it is washed, peeled, chopped, and cooked if necessary.

Step 4: Fill the jars

- Heat the jars in simmering water to keep them warm.
- Place the canning funnel on top of a jar and carefully ladle the prepared food into the jar, leaving the recommended headspace mentioned in the recipe.
- Use the bubble remover or non-metallic spatula to remove air bubbles by sliding it around the inside of the jar.
- Wipe the rim of the jar with a clean, damp cloth to ensure there are no food particles or debris.

Step 5: Apply lids and bands

- Remove a lid from the hot water and place it on top of the jar, making sure the sealing compound is facing down.
- Screw the band on the jar until it's fingertip tight. Do not overtighten.

Step 6: Prepare the pressure canner

- Fill the pressure canner with the recommended amount of water as stated in the canner's instructions. Usually, it's around 2 to 3 inches of water.
- Place the canning rack at the bottom of the canner.
- Ensure the vent or petcock is clean and clear of any obstructions.

Step 7: Load the jars into the canner

- Carefully place the filled jars onto the

canning rack inside the pressure canner, ensuring they don't touch the sides of the canner or each other.
- Secure the lid on the pressure canner, following the manufacturer's instructions.

Step 8: Start the canning process

- Turn on the heat and gradually increase it until steam starts to escape from the vent or petcock.
- Allow steam to vent for 10 minutes to ensure the canner is properly purged of air.
- Close the vent or petcock to build pressure inside the canner.

Step 9: Monitor and adjust pressure

- Watch the pressure gauge closely and adjust the heat to maintain the recommended pressure for your recipe.
- Follow the processing time indicated in the recipe for the specific food being canned.

Step 10: Finish canning and cool down

- When the processing time is complete, turn off the heat and allow the pressure canner to cool naturally.
- Do not force-cool or remove the pressure canner's lid until the pressure has returned to zero and the canner has depressurized completely.

Step 11: Remove the jars

- Once depressurized, open the vent or petcock and wait an additional 10 minutes.
- Carefully remove the lid, tilting it away from your face to avoid steam.
- Use a jar lifter to remove the jars and place them on a towel or cooling rack, leaving space between them.
- Allow the jars to cool undisturbed for 12 to 24 hours. During this time, you may hear a popping sound, indicating that the jars are properly sealed.

Step 12: Check for proper seals

- After the cooling period, check the jars for proper seals. Press down on the center of each lid to ensure it doesn't move or make a popping sound. A properly sealed lid should be concave and not flex when pressed.

Step 13: Store and label the jars

- Wipe the jars clean to remove any residue.
- Label each jar with the contents and the date of canning.
- Store the jars in a cool, dark, and dry place. Properly sealed jars can be stored for up to a year or more, but it's best to consume home-canned foods within one year for optimal quality.

Step 14: Deal with unsealed jars

- If you find any jars that haven't properly sealed, refrigerate them immediately and consume the contents within a few days. Alternatively, you can reprocess the jar using a new lid and following the canning process again.

That's it! By following these steps, you can safely pressure can a variety of foods for long-term storage. Remember to always use reliable recipes and follow proper canning techniques to ensure the safety and quality of your home-canned products.

Preparing the Recipe

There are numerous recipes that can be safely prepared using pressure canning. Here are a few examples of popular recipes for pressure canning:

1. Tomato Sauce:

Ingredients:

- Tomatoes
- onions
- garlic
- herbs (such as basil or oregano)
- salt
- lemon juice (for acidity).

Instructions:

Peel and chop tomatoes. Sauté onions and garlic in a pot, then add tomatoes and herbs. Simmer until thickened. Add salt and lemon juice. Fill jars with sauce, leaving headspace. Process in a pressure canner according to the recommended time for your altitude

2. Vegetable Soup:

Ingredients:

Assorted vegetables (carrots, peas, green beans, corn, potatoes, etc.), broth or water, herbs, salt.

Instructions:

Prepare and chop vegetables. In a large pot, combine vegetables, broth or water, herbs, and salt. Simmer until vegetables are tender. Ladle hot soup into jars, leaving headspace. Process in a pressure canner according to the recommended time for your altitude.

3. Pickled Cucumbers:

Ingredients:

Cucumbers, vinegar, water, sugar, salt, dill seeds, garlic cloves.

Instructions:

Wash and slice cucumbers. In a saucepan, combine vinegar, water, sugar, and salt. Bring to a boil, stirring until sugar and salt dissolve. In each jar, place dill seeds and garlic cloves, then pack cucumber slices tightly. Pour hot pickling liquid over cucumbers, leaving headspace. Process in a pressure canner according to the recommended time for your altitude.

4. Chili Con Carne:

Ingredients:

Ground beef, kidney beans, diced tomatoes, onions, garlic, chili powder, cumin, salt.

Instructions:

Brown ground beef in a pot, then add onions and garlic. Cook until onions are translucent. Add kidney beans, diced tomatoes, chili powder, cumin, and salt. Simmer for about 15-20 minutes. Fill jars with chili, leaving headspace. Process in a pressure canner according to the recommended time for your altitude.

5. Applesauce:

Ingredients:

Apples, water, sugar (optional), lemon juice.

Instructions:

Peel, core, and chop apples. In a pot, combine apples, water, and sugar (if desired). Cook until apples are soft and mushy. Add lemon juice for flavor and to maintain acidity. Puree the mixture or leave it chunky. Fill jars with applesauce, leaving headspace. Process in a pressure canner according to the recommended time for your altitude.

6. Green Beans:

Ingredients:

Fresh green beans, water, salt.

Instructions:

Wash and trim green beans. Fill a large pot with water and bring it to a boil. Blanch the green beans in boiling water for 2 minutes. Drain and pack the beans tightly into jars, leaving headspace. Add boiling water and salt to each jar, covering the beans. Process in a pressure canner according to the recommended time for your altitude.

7. Chicken Stock:

Ingredients:

Chicken bones or carcass, onions, carrots, celery, garlic, bay leaves, peppercorns, salt.

Instructions:

Place chicken bones or carcass in a large pot. Add onions, carrots, celery, garlic, bay leaves, peppercorns, and salt. Cover with water. Bring to a boil, then reduce heat and simmer for several hours. Strain the stock to remove solids. Fill jars with hot stock, leaving headspace. Process in a pressure canner according to the recommended time for your altitude.

Remember to adjust processing times based on your altitude and follow safe canning practices to ensure food safety. Always refer to reliable canning resources for tested recipes and guidelines specific to pressure canning.

Preparing Jars and Lids

Step 1: Gather your equipment

- Pressure canner
- Canning jars
- Canning lids and bands
- Jar lifter
- Canning funnel
- Clean dish towels or paper towels
- Boiling water or dishwasher (optional)
- Clean, hot water

Step 2: Inspect your jars

- Examine each jar for cracks, chips, or other damage.
- Discard any jars with visible defects as they may not seal properly during canning.

Step 3: Clean the jars

- Wash the jars thoroughly with warm, soapy water.
- Use a bottle brush to clean the inside of the jars, especially if they have narrow openings.
- Rinse the jars well to remove any soap residue.

Step 4: Sanitize the jars

1. There are two methods for sanitizing jars:

- a. Boiling water method: Place the jars in a large pot filled with enough water to cover them completely. Bring the water to a boil and let the jars boil for 10 minutes. Remove the jars from the water using a jar lifter and place them on a clean

dish towel or paper towel to dry.
- b. Dishwasher method: If your dishwasher has a sanitizing cycle, you can place the jars in the dishwasher and run a cycle. Make sure the jars are placed securely to avoid breakage.

Step 5: Prepare the lids and bands

- While the jars are being sanitized, prepare the lids and bands.
- Place the lids in a small saucepan and cover them with water. Heat the water until it is steaming hot, but not boiling. Keep the lids in the hot water until you are ready to use them.
- The bands do not need to be heated, but make sure they are clean.

Step 6: Fill the jars

- Once the jars are dry, use a canning funnel to fill them with your prepared food, leaving the recommended headspace for the specific recipe you are using. Wipe the rims of the jars with a clean, damp cloth to remove any food particles or liquid that could prevent a proper seal.

Step 7: Apply the lids and bands

- Remove a lid from the hot water using a magnetic lid lifter or tongs. Place the lid on the jar, ensuring it is centered. Screw the band on finger-tight. Do not overtighten.

Step 8: Load the jars into the pressure canner

- Follow the manufacturer's instructions for your specific pressure canner.
- Place the filled jars into the canner, using a jar lifter to prevent burns.
- Make sure the jars are spaced apart and not touching each other or the sides of the canner.

Step 9: Process the jars

- Close and lock the lid of the pressure canner according to the manufacturer's instructions.
- Adjust the heat to achieve the

recommended pressure for your recipe.
- Process the jars for the specified amount of time, starting the timer once the desired pressure is reached.

Step 10: Release pressure and remove jars

- Once the processing time is complete, turn off the heat and let the pressure canner cool down naturally.
- Do not force-cool or open the canner until the pressure has returned to zero and the canner is completely depressurized.
- Carefully remove the jars from the canner using a jar lifter and place them on a towel-lined countertop.
- Let the jars cool undisturbed for 12 to 24 hours.

Step 11: Check the seals

- After the jars have cooled, check the seals by pressing down on the center of each lid.
- If the lid springs back, it did not properly seal. In this case, refrigerate the jar and consume its contents within a few days.
- If the lid is firmly sucked down and does not move, it indicates a proper seal. You can proceed with storing the jars.

Step 12: Store the jars

- Remove the metal bands from the sealed jars. This prevents rusting and allows you to detect any spoiled or unsealed jars easily.
- Label the jars with the contents and the date of canning.
- Store the jars in a cool, dry, and dark place such as a pantry or cellar. Properly sealed jars can be stored for up to one year or according to the specific recommendations of your recipe.

Following these steps will ensure that your jars and lids are properly prepared for pressure canning, allowing you to safely preserve your food. Remember to always consult reliable canning resources and recipes for specific processing times and guidelines.

Filling Jars and Removing Air Bubbles

Pressure canning is a popular method for preserving various foods such as vegetables, fruits, soups, and meats. When using a pressure canner, it is essential to fill jars properly and remove any air bubbles to ensure safe and effective preservation. This guide will walk you through the step-by-step process of filling jars and removing air bubbles during pressure canning.

Equipment and Supplies Needed:

- Pressure canner
- Canning jars with appropriate lids and bands
- Jar lifter
- Canning funnel
- Bubble remover or non-metallic utensil
- Clean towels
- Boiling water or canning liquid
- Timer
- Canning recipe and ingredients

Step 1: Prepare the Jars

1. Start by inspecting your canning jars for any cracks, chips, or defects. Discard any damaged jars as they may compromise the seal.

2. Wash the jars, lids, and bands with hot, soapy water. Rinse them thoroughly to remove any soap residue.

Step 2: Preheat the Jars (Optional)

1. If your canning recipe requires processing for more than 10 minutes, preheat the jars before filling them. This helps prevent thermal shock and potential jar breakage.

2. Place the cleaned jars in a large pot filled with hot water. Bring the water to a simmer (180°F/82°C), but do not boil.

3. Keep the jars in the hot water until ready to use.

Step 3: Prepare the Canning Liquid or Brine

1. Follow your specific canning recipe to prepare the appropriate canning liquid or brine. This may include water, vinegar, salt, sugar, or a combination of ingredients.

2. Heat the canning liquid or brine in a separate pot, but do not boil it. Keep it hot until you are ready to fill the jars.

Step 4: Fill the Jars

1. Place the canning funnel on top of a jar.

2. Ladle the hot canning liquid or brine into the jar, leaving the recommended headspace specified in your recipe. Headspace is the distance between the top of the food or liquid and the rim of the jar.

3. Use a non-metallic utensil or bubble remover to slide down the sides of the jar, gently removing any air bubbles. This helps ensure proper heat penetration and prevents spoilage.

4. Continue filling the jar with the liquid or brine, maintaining the recommended headspace.

5. Wipe the rim of the jar clean with a clean, damp towel to remove any spills or residue. A clean rim ensures a proper seal.

Step 5: Apply the Lids and Bands

1. Remove a lid from the hot water and place it on the jar's rim. Ensure the sealing compound on the lid is facing down.

2. Secure the lid in place with a band, tightening it until it is finger-tight. Do not over-tighten.

3. Repeat this process for each jar, working quickly to maintain the jars' heat.

Step 6: Load the Jars into the Pressure Canner

1. Follow the manufacturer's instructions for your specific pressure canner to add the appropriate amount of water to the canner.

2. Place the filled jars on the canning rack, ensuring they are upright and not touching each other or the sides of the canner.

3. Secure the lid of the pressure canner following the manufacturer's instructions.

Step 7: Process the Jars

1. Heat the pressure canner according to the instructions specific to your canner model. Ensure you achieve and maintain the Process of the Jars

2. Once the pressure canner reaches the recommended pressure for your recipe, start the timer for the required processing time.

3. Maintain a consistent pressure throughout the processing time by adjusting the heat as necessary.

4. Monitor the pressure gauge or indicator to ensure it remains within the specified range.

5. When the processing time is complete, turn off the heat and allow the pressure canner to cool down naturally. Do not attempt to force-cool the canner.

Step 8: Remove Jars from the Canner

1. After the pressure has fully released and the pressure gauge or indicator shows zero pressure, carefully unlock and remove the canner lid.

2. Using a jar lifter, lift the jars out of the canner, keeping them upright to avoid disturbing the seals.

3. Place the hot jars on a towel-lined surface or a cooling rack, leaving space between them for air circulation.

4. Let the jars cool undisturbed for 12 to 24 hours. During this time, you may hear the lids make a popping sound as they seal.

Step 9: Check Seals and Store

1. After the cooling period, check the seals by pressing the center of each lid. If the lid springs back, it did not seal properly. In this case, refrigerate and consume the contents within a few days or reprocess the jar using a new lid.

2. Remove the bands from the sealed jars. Wipe the jars clean to remove any residue.

3. Label each jar with the contents and the date of processing.

4. Store the jars in a cool, dark, and dry place. Properly sealed

and processed jars can be stored for up to a year or as recommended by your recipe.

Additional Tips:

1. Follow tested and reliable canning recipes from trusted sources to ensure food safety.

2. Adjust processing times and pressure according to your altitude, if necessary.

3. Do not use jars with cracks, chips, or defects, as they may fail during processing.

4. Always use new, undamaged lids to ensure a proper seal.

5. Use caution when working with hot jars and liquids to avoid burns.

By following these steps, you can confidently fill jars and remove air bubbles during pressure canning, ensuring the safe and successful preservation of your favorite foods.

CHAPTER 5

Pickling and Fermenting

Some overlap between fermentation and pickling can lead to confusion.

In any case, you can prepare fermented cucumber pickles or pickled cucumber pickles. But do cucumber pickles that have been fermented constitute "fermented or pickled? This article examines the overlap between these two methods of food preservation and preparation to provide answers to this question and others.

In brief, here is what you should keep in mind: Pickling involves soaking foods in an acidic liquid to achieve a sour flavor, whereas fermentation produces a sour flavor as a result of a chemical reaction between a food's sugars and naturally present microbes — without the addition of acid.

The Specification of Pickled and Fermented Foods

Pickling: A food that has been pickled has been preserved in a brine of equal parts acid and water with salt. The brine may consist of salt or salty water, while the acid is typically vinegar or an acidic fluid such as lemon juice. Because they are typically heated for sterilization and preservation purposes during canning, non-fermented pickled foods do not provide the probiotic and enzymatic benefits of fermented foods. However, when heated and packaged in a jar, pickled foods can be stored at room temperature for a much longer duration than fermented foods.

Bacteria are responsible for the preservation of fermented foods. Lactobacillus, which consumes natural sugars and carbohydrates and generates lactic acid, is one of the most prevalent types of bacteria. This lactic acid helps preserve and flavor the food. Probiotics and digestive enzymes are present in foods that have been fermented at home. These foods must be refrigerated or stored in a root cellar or other cold location.

Overlap between the two

Some pickles are fermented, and some fermented foods are pickled, but not all pickles and fermented foods are fermented and pickled, respectively. It seems perplexing at first, but it becomes clearer once we examine some examples.

Fermented instead of preserved: The following fermented foods are not pickled: yogurt, sourdough bread, beer, kefir, cheese, kombucha, and sour cream. They are not preserved in an acidic medium, nor does the fermentation procedure produce enough acid to qualify them as pickled. These are mostly straightforward examples, as you would not assume that a loaf of sourdough bread had been marinated based on its appearance alone.

However, if you are unfamiliar with kombucha, a fermented beverage, you may be perplexed. It is a non-salty liquid that, if allowed to ferment for an extended period of time, can acquire a vinegary flavor. What is it? The substance is fermented. Bacteria in the SCOBY consume the sugars in the tea, thereby imparting a vinegar-like flavor. In addition, this 2-gallon keg and spigot are perfect for fermenting and continuous brewing of kombucha beverages. Please visit our website for comprehensive kombucha-related information.

Pickled, not fermented: Store-bought pickles and other foods that have been quickly pickled are not fermented foods. These are somewhat more difficult to identify than the previous group, but they lack the distinct flavor of fermented foods. If you're interested, our definitive canning kit for pickling and preserving non-fermented foods has you covered.

Some edibles are pickled and fermented simultaneously. This category includes foods such as sauerkraut, pickled cucumbers, and kimchi. Surstromming, or Swedish sour herring, is simultaneously preserved and fermented. In each of these foods, a salty brine is used to eliminate harmful microorganisms, thereby pickling the food. The nonpathogenic bacteria then ferment the food, resulting in fermented and pickled food. If you are interested in fermenting your own food, this kit contains everything you need to get started.

Differences between Fermentation and Pickling

TEMPERATURE

Fermented ingredients will be our first topic. All fermented foods rely on microorganisms to alter their physical state, enhance their flavor, and preserve them for future consumption. These bacteria flourish at specific temperatures, and depending on whether you are using mesophilic or thermophilic cultures, they may perish if exposed to excessive heat.

Mesophilic bacteria flourish between 68°F and 113°F, whereas thermophilic bacteria flourish between 106°F and 254°F. For this reason, this electric yogurt maker is so useful during the yogurt-making procedure.

Throughout the fermentation process, it maintains the milk at a constant temperature. Some fermented foods (such as sourdough bread during the baking process) incorporate heat into the formulation to kill the bacteria.

In contrast, in fermented foods such as kimchi, sauerkraut, and even fermented pickles, the bacteria and enzymes continue to exist and only become quiescent when the food is chilled or refrigerated. In fact, these foods must be refrigerated or stored below 45 degrees Fahrenheit.

Much less temperature-sensitive are pickled edibles. Frequently, they are canned, which involves bringing them to a boil and maintaining them there for a predetermined period. This procedure would eliminate mesophilic bacteria, but it also makes these preserved foods shelf-stable at room temperature.

DESIRED RESULT

Why choose marinating instead of fermentation, or vice versa? Pickling produces foods that can be stored at room temperature for extended periods of time. Fermenting can produce a greater diversity of foods with increased health benefits, such as enzymes and probiotics, but most fermented foods must be refrigerated and have a shelf life of no more than six months to one year, with the exception of kombucha, which is never spoiled.

Pickling Techniques and Tips

Pickling is a method for preserving the season's bounty. Consult our advice, pickling techniques, and pickling recipes.

Adding acid (vinegar or lemon juice) to a low-acid product in order to reduce its pH to 4.6 or lower is the process of pickling.

All fruits besides figs, the majority of tomatoes, fermented and preserved vegetables, relishes, jams, jellies, and marmalades are acidic foods.

PICKLING TIPS

- When making pickles, produce must be fresh. Produce that has been varnished should be avoided.
- Select the freshest, most homogenous produce.
- Scrub food properly. Ensure that you remove and discard a 14-inch slice from the blossom end of fresh cucumbers. Blossoms may contain an enzyme that softens pickles excessively.
- Use marinating or preserving salt, not iodized table salt! Pickling salt is additive-free. Iodized salt causes the brine to become cloudy and may alter the color and texture of the vegetables, as well as leave residue at the bottom of the jars.
- For optimal results, use 5 percent-acid white distilled or cider vinegar, when a pale color is desired, such as with fruits and cauliflower, white vinegar should be used.
- For crispier pickles, place the vegetables (whole or sliced) in a large dish and sprinkle with pickling salt. In a quiet location, cover and leave overnight. Before pickling or canning as usual, discard the liquid and rinse and dry the vegetables. The salt

helps remove moisture from the vegetables, making them crispier.
- Because the proportion of fresh food to other ingredients affects flavor and in many cases, food safety, it is important to measure or weigh ingredients precisely. Here are the parameters for pickling:

PICKLING MEASURES

Pickling salt	1 pound = 1-⅓ cup
Granulated sugar	1 pound = 2 cups
Brown sugar	1 pound = 2-¼ to 2-¾ cups, firmly packed
Fresh herbs	1 tablespoon = ½ teaspoon crushed dried herbs

- Empty vessels must be sterilized. Do not use recycled commercial vessels or home-canning jars of outdated design. They may shatter during the canning procedure.
- For a secure seal, use new container lids. Screw bands should be removed from processed jars that are being stored to prevent corrosion. Once the jars have cooled and been sealed, they are readily removable and reusable.
- Always clear the rim of the jar after filling and just before placing the lid to ensure a good seal.
- Process jars in a canner with boiling water for the specified amount of time (a canner is a large standard-size kettle with a jar rack, designed for heat-processing 7-quart jars or 8- to 9-pint jars in boiling water).

- Label and date your jars and store them in a clean, cool, dark, and dry location, such as a pantry, cupboard, or cellar. Avoid storing in humid areas!
- Wait at least three weeks prior to using pickles to enable them to mellow.

Fermentation Basics and Guidelines

During all phases of the fermentation process, it is crucial that good manufacturing practices, such as cleanliness and appropriate hand washing, are adhered to with extreme precision. These methods include:

- During preparation, thoroughly cleanse all produce, hands, cutting implements and boards, and containers.
- Choose vegetables that are healthy, undamaged, of uniform size, and at the appropriate level of ripeness.
- During fermentation, the vessel must be secured.
- Culture should never be neglected.
- Fermentation requires an oxygen-free environment.
- During fermentation, the product must be covered with liquid to prevent oxygen exposure. To exclude oxygen and assure anaerobic conditions, the fermentation vessel must be sealed.

- If an item becomes discolored (pink or dark) it must be discarded. This discoloration represents spoilage.
- Temperature and pH must be meticulously recorded throughout production.
- Calibrations of equipment must be performed and documented.
- Depending on the type of product, keep records for two years.
- After fermentation is complete, refrigerate the product (below 40 degrees Fahrenheit).
- The processing of fermented foods for shelf stability necessitates product testing by a process authority to determine a product-specific thermal process.
- The FDA does not require registration for the sale of fermented foods, as they are not considered acidic.

Pickling and Fermentation Recipes

Pickling recipes

- Always use vegetables that are as fresh as possible to preserve their texture.
- Experiment and enjoy yourself while you discover your new favorite spice combinations. A little chili, mustard, or kaffir lime leaves can go a long way.

- Use kosher, sea, or pickling salt instead of regular table salt, which contains anti-caking agents like iodine that can cloud brines and inhibit the development of beneficial bacteria during fermentation.
- You can also flavor vinegars and brines by adding elderflower, shiso, liquorice, and pineapple weed.
- Don't be alarmed if your brined garlic turns blue! The pickle will not be harmed.

Fermentation Recipes

It may seem counterintuitive to cover fresh ingredients in salt and leave them out of the refrigerator for several days or weeks. However, it is a safe and straightforward method for creating intense flavors that can then be incorporated into exceptional dishes.

This collection of fermentation recipes will get you well on your way to creating healthy, delicious ferments and provide some inspiration for how to use them in cookery. Begin with kimchi, selecting either the traditional Korean cabbage kimchi or one prepared with barley and black pepper. In addition, sauerkraut and miso must be prepared from fresh.

For actual dishes, Anna Hansen's lamb neck with fennel kimchi and Pollyanna Coupland's mushroom and chestnut paté with tarragon and fermented cranberries will not disappoint. Try Joey O'Hare's fermented tomato salsa for a condiment with a difference.

Before using any vessels or equipment for food preservation, they must be thoroughly scrubbed and sanitized. Also, be sure to adhere to the precise ratios of salt listed; too much or too little salt will have a significant impact on the fermentation process.

CHAPTER 6

Jams, Jellies, and Preserves

Fruit spreads always include the following four components: fruit, acid, pectin, and sugar. Nevertheless, the quantity of each ingredient used distinguishes jams, jellies, and preserves. Different concentrations of acid, pectin, and fruit have a significant impact on consistency and produce distinct outcomes.

JAMS

Jams have a middle-of-the-road consistency, which makes them ideal for pairing with baked brie or spreading on toast. When cooked with sugar, this condiment made from pulverized or chopped fruits typically acquires a semi-solid but still wiggly consistency but does not gel. Due to the remaining fruit pulp, jam should be at least slightly opaque with visible fruit fragments.

JELLIES

Jelly is distinguished by its dearth of fruit pulp and its transparency. The only ingredient in this spread is citrus juice. To make a jelly firm, fruits rich in pectin and acid (such as currants and lemons) are simmered with sugar to form a gel. However, many fruits require additional pectin or acid in order to attain gelatin status. Jellies, specifically grape and apricot, are a delectable addition to English muffins and the heroes of stuffed French toast!

PRESERVES

The thickest of the three spreads, preserves are made from whole fruits or small pieces of fruit that are frequently suspended in a slightly thickened syrup or in the jelly itself. This fruit spread pairs well with cheese and lends a citrusy kick to any charcuterie platter.

In some fruit preparations, the distinction between jams, jellies, and preserves is less distinct. Some spreads share characteristics with more than one category or blur the boundaries between the three, which expands the ways in which jams and spreads can be utilized.

Sohnrey Family Foods offers spreads for all occasions, from lusciously dense jams to take your morning toast to the next level to thinner jellies that complement English muffins and pancakes.

Introduction to Making Jams, Jellies, and Preserves

A significant category of preserved fruit products are jams, jellies, and marmalades. Apple jam, pineapple jam, strawberry jam, and mixed fruit jam made with the puree of two or more fruits are widely available. Likewise, guava jelly and orange marmalade are examples of such products.

The fruit is cooked in a heavy sugar solution until it becomes tender and translucent, either whole or in large chunks. A candied fruit, such as petha candy or ginger candy, is a fruit that has been saturated with cane sugar and glucose, then drained and dried. In addition, candied fruit covered or coated with a thin, translucent sugar coating that imparts a glossy appearance is known as "glazed fruit. When candied fruit is coated with sugar crystals by rolling it in powdered sugar or by allowing the sugar crystals from glucose syrup to deposit on it, the fruit becomes crystallized. These products are preserved through the use of a high concentration of sugar. The commercial products in this category include Petha candy, Aonla preserve, apple rings, candied citrus segments, ginger candy, ginger in syrup, bael, pineapple, and carrot preserve.

1. Jam: Jam is made by boiling fruit pulp with a sufficient amount of sugar until it reaches a consistency that is viscous and firm enough to hold fruit tissues in place. The method for making jam and jelly is identical, with the exception that fruit puree and chunks are used to make jam, whereas fruit extract is used to make jelly. The final product must contain a minimum of 68 percent (w/w) soluble solids in accordance with FPO specifications.

Procedure for jam preparation

The fruit is thoroughly cleansed to eliminate any clinging dust and grime. Depending on the variety of fruit, the fruit is then subjected to a preliminary treatment.

Strawberries are squashed between rollers, while raspberries are steamed, crushed, and sieved to remove their tough cores.

The stones are removed from plums, peaches, and apricots by passing them through a sieve with a coarse mesh after softening them with a small amount of water.

After softening the fruit by boiling it with a small amount of water, the pulper can be used to extract the pulp from the fruit.

Peel and core pears before cutting them into small segments.

Mangoes are peeled, the stones are removed, and the sliced

fruit is then passed through a pulper.

Peeling, slicing, and core-punching pineapples The slices are then cut into smaller pieces and passed through a screw-type crusher to obtain a pulp coarse enough for producing jam.

When two or more fruits or fruit pulps are combined in the proper proportions for the preparation of jam, the result is called mixed fruit jam.

Typically, 55 parts of cane sugar (sucrose) are added for every 45 parts of fruit when making jam. In order to prevent crystallization of sugar during storage, the prepared jam should contain 30 to 50 percent inverted sugar. If the percentage of invert sugar (reducing sugar) is less than 30 percent, jam crystallizes, and if it is greater than 50 percent, it transforms into a mass resembling honey due to the formation of small glucose crystals. Sugar should not be added excessively, as jam with high total soluble solids becomes sticky and gummy.

Addition of acid, color, and flavor: For the production of jam, citric, tartaric, or malic acids are utilized to supplement the acidity of the fruit. To achieve the proper combination of pectin, sugar, and acid for jam setting, acid must be added to fruits that are acid-deficient. Before sugar is added, the pH of the fruit juice and pectin mixture should be 3.0. Only edible food colorings should be used, and they should be added at the end of the boiling process. At the conclusion of cooking and just prior to packaging, flavors are added.

To facilitate pulping, the fruit and a small amount of water are placed in a saucepan and brought to a boil. It is then cooked until the pectin is released. Following the addition of sugar, the mixture is boiled in order to concentrate the soluble solids to approximately 68.5% and to allow for the required amount of sugar inversion. A steam-jacketed kettle or a stainless steel or aluminum boiling pan may be utilized for boiling. Jam is prepared at a lower temperature (65–750 °C) by boiling in a vacuum pan under reduced pressure to minimize unfavorable changes and preserve vitamins.

End Point: The end point can be determined with a jelmeter test.

Typically, for fruits that are relatively high in pectin, the weight of the finished jam is 1.5 times (1 1/2 times) the amount of sugar used. At sea level, the boiling point of jam with 68.5% soluble solids is 1050°C. It ought to produce a specific amount of finished jam.

The jam is packed in sterile glass jars for storage. It should be noted that unless the jars are stored in a relatively cool location, the jam will shrink due to the evaporation of moisture. If jam is made from fresh, unsulfurized fruit pulp, it is recommended to add 40 ppm of sulfur dioxide in the form of potassium meta-bi-sulfite, which is allowed by law. The surface of the cooled jam in the glass jar can be coated with a layer of molten paraffin wax, which solidifies upon cooling.

This serves as a safeguard against any potential mold growth on the jam's surface.

2. Making JELLY involves boiling fruit with or without water, straining the extract, combining the clear extract with sugar, and then boiling the mixture until it solidifies into a clear gel. The jelly should be transparent, well-set but not overly rigid, and possess the flavor of the fruit. It should be of a pleasing hue and retain its form with a smooth, cut surface. Pectin is the most essential component in the preparation of jellies. The cell wall of fruits contains pectin. To obtain a high-quality jelly, pectin-rich but acid-deficient fruits should be chosen.

Procedure for jelly preparation

Selection of fruits: The fruits should be sufficiently ripe but not overripe, and they should have excellent flavor. Slightly under-ripe fruit yields more pectin than over-ripe fruit, as during maturation the pectin present is decomposed into pectic acid, which does not form a jelly with acid and sugar. The amount of pectin extracted from a fruit depends on the degree of disintegration of its protection during the heating process.

Pectin requirement: Usually 0.5 to 1 percent of pectin in the extract is sufficient to produce a good jelly. If the pectin content is in excess, a firm and tough jelly is formed, and if it is less, the jelly may fail to set. Pectin, sugar, acid, and water are the four essential constituents of a jelly and must be present in approximately the following proportions:

- Pectin, 1 percent
- Sugar, 60 to 65 percent
- Fruit acid, 1 percent
- Water, 33 to 38 percent

However, the exact proportion of sugar depends on the pectin grade.

Pectin grades: Grades of pectin mean the weight of sugar required to set one gram of pectin under suitable conditions to form a satisfactory jelly. e.g. 100-grade pectin means 100g of sugar is required for the setting of 1 g of pectin.

Basic Fruit Preserving Techniques

When you have a bountiful harvest or reside close enough to farms to take advantage of farmer's markets, you'll want to put every last tomato and peach to good use. Preserving the harvest can allow you to savor the results of your labor for several months. There are various techniques for preserving fruits, vegetables, and botanicals. The method you select will depend on the variety of fruit or vegetable you're preserving as well as your level of ambition.

STORING

Storing your bounty is the simplest way to preserve it, but the shelf life of most vegetables is short. Longevity is greatest for root vegetables and vegetables that can be preserved, such as onions and winter squash.

Storage Fundamentals:

- Store only completely mature and healthy vegetables. Any dented or immature vegetables must be consumed fresh or preserved in another way.
- Before freezing vegetables, remove the soil and allow the exterior to air out.
- Leave a few inches of stem on winter squash and trim the verdant apex of root vegetables to about an inch.

FREEZING

Numerous vegetables are freezer-stable. This can be the most effective method for preserving nutrients, color, texture, and flavor when blanched and frozen immediately after harvest. Most vegetables can be stored in the freezer for 8 to 12 weeks.

Guidelines for Freezing

- After packaging food, freeze it immediately.
- Keep refrigeration temperatures at 0 degrees F. or lower. To accelerate the chilling process, you can set your freezer to -10 degrees Fahrenheit the day before.

- Do not attempt to fill your freezer full of unfrozen produce. This will only decrease the freezer's temperature and increase the time required for the produce to cool.

CANNING

Canning is an excellent method for preserving fruits and vegetables with a high water content, such as tomatoes, mushrooms, beans, and apricots, but it is imperative that you strictly adhere to the canning instructions.

Tips for Canning:

- Utilize clean jars with brand-new closures.
- For the specified period of time, process in scalding water or a pressure canner.

Drying fruits, vegetables, and herbs is also a simple process that can be accomplished without special apparatus or sped up by using an oven or dehydrator. By employing these techniques, one can dry fruits, grains, jerky, leather, and even popcorn.

Guidelines for Drying:

- To prevent decomposition, provide adequate airflow while drying.
- Ensure that the fruits and vegetables are ripe and free of disease.

PICKLING

Many vegetables and fruits, including peppers, cauliflower, apples, and pears, can be pickled and preserved in this way. Pickling is also used to create relishes.

Basic Pickling Tips:

- Always use an established recipe. Even in vinegar, deterioration can happen. The boiling-water method of canning pickled products prevents deterioration even further.
- Before processing, choose only fruits and vegetables that are free of disease and thoroughly cleanse them.

JAMS AND JELLIES

Producing preserves and jellies is the most aromatic method of food preservation.

Basic Guidelines for Preparing Jams and Jellies:

- Jelly made from the ripest, most succulent produce is superior.
- For fruits to coalesce, the level of acidity must be optimal. Low-acid products are given lemon juice.
- Recipe sugar proportions should not be altered. Sugar aids in fruit preservation and gelling.

Creating Jams, Jellies, and Preserves with Pectin

Pectin is a gelling agent, which means that it causes substances to gel, such as our jelly. It occurs naturally in some fruits but is absent in others, so we must keep this in mind when preparing our preserves and add as necessary.

PECTIN JAM GELATIN

Pectin for creating jam at home can be purchased in stores. It is available in either liquid form in a container or powder form in sachets.

Typically, the powdered form is combined with sugar prior to simmering.

The commercial liquid stock is added after the sugar has been boiled, unlike the pectin that occurs naturally in the fruit.

Useful quantity of pectin

You can adjust the suggested quantity. If, for instance, the instructions on the Silver Spoon powdered form state, "Use 13g of pectin powder per kilogram of sugar," but you know that your jam contains only a slight deficiency in pectin, you can reduce the quantity by half to prevent the jam from setting too solidly.

It is especially difficult to gauge levels when preparing a mixed fruit jam.

Additionally, pectin-added marmalade sugar is available for purchase. Not to be confused with preservation sugar which does not contain added pectin but is formulated to reduce the formation of scum during the jam-making process.

Pectin Levels in Fruits

High-Pectin Fruits:

- Blackcurrants
- Cranberries
- Damsons
- Plums
- Gooseberries

- Redcurrants
- Cooking Apples
- Quince

Fresh apricots, containing medium pectin:

- Greengages
- Loganberries
- Raspberries
- Early-season blackberry

Fruits with Low Pectin Levels

- Blackberries (late seasonCherries
- Elderberries
- Medlars
- Pears
- Rhubarb
- Strawberries

Stock prepared at home

You can create your own pectin stock from cooking or crab apples if you so choose. Crab pears are a fantastic ingredient for this stock. Redcurrants and gooseberries can also be utilized to produce pectin stock.

Take 1.8 kilograms (4 pounds) of rinsed cooking apples or crab apples. Place the sliced vegetables into a stainless steel or enamel saucepan. Peeling, coring, and removing the seeds are unnecessary. Just add sufficient water to cover and bring to a simmer. Simmer until the apples are mushy, then strain through a metal sieve, forcing most of the pulp into a separate saucepan.

The next day, reheat and reduce the liquid by half.

Your homemade stock can be refrigerated for several days. You can refrigerate it, but doing so diminishes its efficacy. You can also store your stock in bottles.

Special Jam and Jelly Recipes

Ah, marmalade. It is the perfect vehicle for spreading on your beloved sandwich (PB&J, of course) and morning toast. However, homemade preserves and jellies can be utilized for more than just bread. You can use distinctive jam flavors such as tomato-basil, carrot cake, and jasmine tea as a base for meats, appetizers, and more.

We have an abundance of marmalade and jam recipes to preserve your produce, whether you are an experienced canner or a novice. Classics such as strawberry jam are available, but we're confident that you'll find our unique jam flavor combinations particularly appealing.

1. Very Berry Rhubarb Jam

When you begin the day with a delectable combination of berries and rhubarb, life is simple (and delicious). Want further persuasion? As a time-saving shortcut, we use blueberry pie filling.

2. Strawberry Jam

Enjoy this flavor throughout the entire year. Each batch of this traditional homemade jam recipe contains three quarts of ripe, juicy strawberries, enough to keep you beaming until the next berry season.

3. Raspberry jam

There are few things as tasty as raspberry jam and butter on freshly prepared bread. Furthermore, homemade food tastes even better. Personalize your marmalade recipe with simple additions like lemon, nutmeg, and fresh ginger.

Always cleanse fruits and vegetables thoroughly before incorporating them into recipes.

4. Strawberry-Chia Seed Jam

This marmalade recipe incorporates chia seeds to great effect. When combined with liquid (in this case, berries and honey), these microscopic particles thicken the mixture naturally.

Chia seeds are an outstanding source of fiber, protein, and omega-3 fatty acids.

5. Rhubarb and Rose Petal Jam

The delicate, delectable flavor of rose petals complements the sourness of fresh rhubarb. When used in baked goods such as homemade donuts or freshly baked scones, this distinctive jam recipe really shines.

Avoid pesticides by using roses from your own garden, a farmer's market, or a specialty food store.

CHAPTER 7

Salsas, Sauces, and Relishes

Salsas: are typically piquant mixtures of acidic ingredients, such as chopped tomatoes, and low-acid ingredients, such as onions and peppers; however, many salsas also contain fruits and/or other vegetables.

Sauce: Any liquid or semi-liquid condiment consumed with food to enhance its flavor Sauces and purees are made by heating a mixture of vegetables (typically tomato-based), seasonings, salt, and sugar to evaporate water and concentrate the mixture. Occasionally, they contain thickeners to make the substance smooth and velvety. Many sauces contain wheat, maize starch, and other thickeners.

Relish/Chutney: A relish is a cooked, pickled, or minced vegetable or fruit food item that is typically employed as a condiment. Relishes and chutneys are typically served alongside a meal to add flavor as an appetizer or a pickled condiment and are typically made with seasonings, sugar, vinegar, etc.

Concerns Regarding Food Safety: In canned foods such as salsa, relishes, chutneys, and sauces, acidity is one factor that is used to control the proliferation of certain microorganisms. Foodborne illness outbreaks have been linked to a variety of these products' raw constituents, including hot peppers, tomatoes, green onions, and cilantro. Problems may result from improper processing and handling of these goods. Even salsas or sauces with a significant tomato content may have a pH greater than 4.6 and must be acidified as a result. In order to lower the pH, vinegar or other acids can be applied.

This distinction between pH is extremely essential because improperly processed low-acid foods can support the growth of potentially dangerous bacteria such as Clostridium botulinum. In addition to acidity, thermal processing (heat treatment) is employed to ensure the safety and shelf-stability of edibles.

- On a scale from zero to 14, acidity is quantified.
- Acid foods are those with a pH less than or equal to 4.62.

- Examples: lemon juice, vinegar, and some fruits
- Those with a pH greater than 4.6 are considered 'low-acid."
- Meat, milk, and bread are some examples.

Water activity refers to the amount of water in a food that is available for microbial proliferation. On a scale from 0 to 1, it is measured with a water activity meter. Regardless of their acidity, foods with pH values below 0.85 are deemed safe because they do not promote the growth of dangerous microorganisms.

- Because a cracker's water activity is 0.20, it cannot harbor pathogenic microorganisms.
- Cheese's water activity of 0.95 provides microbes with the necessary moist environment for survival.

Although the U.S. Food and Drug Administration's current guidelines for testing acidified foods specify that pH paper can be used to determine the acidity of foods, the Colorado Department of Health and Environment requires the use of a pH meter to measure acidity. Your food product must be tested in a laboratory with a calibrated pH meter before it can be processed and sold in the state of Colorado. Typically, acidity must be determined by analyzing three samples from three distinct volumes.

Good Agricultural and Good Handling Practices (GAP and GHP): In manufacturing, acidification cannot replace hygienic practices and caution. Utilizing good manufacturing practices, the manufacturer must therefore adhere to the strictest hygiene and product safety standards. In addition, a number of the unprocessed ingredients used to create these products, such as hot peppers, tomatoes, green onions, and cilantro, have been linked to outbreaks of foodborne illness. Using good agricultural practices on the farm will prevent the initial contamination of these produce items.

Tomato-Based Salsa Recipes

The majority of salsas made with tomatoes consist of tomatoes, onions, peppers, and seasonings. For home canning in a boiling water bath, you must adhere to research-tested formulas to ensure that the proportion of acidic ingredients is sufficient to ensure food safety.

Salsa: safe canning techniques

- Choose only firm, disease-free, and high-quality produce for canning. Canning is not an option for using overripe or damaged tomatoes, as well as tomatoes from deceased or frost-killed vines, as these may cause the home-canned product to spoil and become unsafe for consumption.
- The safety of salsa requires the addition of acid. Salsa can be made with a combination of tomato varieties and colors, but acid must be added to ensure the product's safety.

North Dakota State University researchers evaluated fourteen tomato cultivars cultivated at a North Dakota research facility. They measured the pH, or acidity, of tomatoes, salsa with lemon juice, and salsa without lemon juice. All 14 tomato varieties examined had a pH greater than 4.62. All salsas with added bottled lemon juice tested well below the required pH level of 4.6 to prevent botulism. All salsas without added lemon juice tested above 4.6 and posed a risk of botulism. This study explains why acid must be added to home-canned tomatoes to reduce pH and prevent botulism.

- Do not reduce the quantity of tomatoes or lemon or lime juice called for in the recipe.

- Utilize dry measuring cups for tomatoes, shallots, and peppers and liquid measuring cups for bottled lemon and lime juice.
- Tomatoes, peppers, and onions should be chopped into 14-inch sections.
- Add no additional peppers, onions, or garlic. You can substitute one variety of pepper for another or reduce the quantity of peppers, onions, and garlic.
- Spices can be adapted to individual preferences without compromising safety.
- Never thicken salsas with cornstarch, flour, or other thickeners prior to canning. Upon opening the salsa, if preferred, add thickeners.
- Always refrigerate homemade salsa canisters that have been opened.

When canning salsa, use only a research-tested recipe.

- Food degradation or foodborne illness could result from attempting to can a recipe that has not been evaluated for safety.
- National Center for Home Food Preserving You can choose whether you want more pepper flavor or onion flavor in your salsa.
- Popular on culinary blogs and social media sites are salsa recipes for canning. The

researchers from the University of Maine evaluated 56 salsa home-canning recipes from 43 blogs and found that 70% of the recipes did not adhere to the USDA's home-canning food safety guidelines.
- Credible and standardized salsa recipes will instruct you to use pint jars and will only provide processing times for pint jars.
- Currently, there are no research-tested guidelines for processing salsa in one-quart jars. No formula exists for extending the processing time for a larger container.

Salsa ingredients

Tomatoes

Which variety of tomato performs best in homemade Salsa:

The quality of salsa will be affected by the type of tomato used

- Italian plum-style or paste tomatoes, such as Roma, generate a salsa with a thicker consistency due to their firmer flesh.
- Salsa becomes thinner and more fluid when tomatoes are sliced. If you use sliced tomatoes, you can thicken your salsa by adding tomato purée or by removing some of the liquid after the tomatoes have been chopped. Never add

flour or cornstarch to salsa prior to canning, as the resulting product could be hazardous.

- Choose tomatoes that are fresh, firm, and ripe at their apex. Utilize only tomatoes without blemishes, fissures, disease, or insect damage. Soft, overripe, or overripe tomatoes with bruises, cracks, blossom end rot, mold, insect damage, or those harvested from frost-killed vines can alter the acidity level of the entire quantity and render it hazardous. Produce that is infected or blemished may contain pathogens. There is a possibility that the processing time is insufficient to eliminate additional microorganisms on spoiled or diseased produce.
- Tomatoes can be used both dried and in a can.
- Roasting tomatoes and incorporating some of the roasted husks enhances the flavor.

By adding tomato purée, salsa can be thickened.

- Never thicken salsa with flour or cornstarch before canning, as this may produce a hazardous product.
- After opening, salsas may also be thickened.

Tomatoes or tomatillos (Mexican shell tomatoes) that are green.

- These may be used in place of or in

combination with scarlet tomatoes.
- There is no need to skin or seed tomatillos.
- The outer coverings must be stripped away.

PEPPERS

Peppers spice up salsa recipes with color and flavor.

Utilize peppers of premium quality.

- Never increase the total quantity of peppers in a recipe.
- One type of pepper can be substituted for another.
- Chilis in a can can substitute for fresh.
- The flavor of peppers ranges from moderate to fiery.

Hot peppers include jalapeno, serrano, cayenne, and habanero and are generally tiny (1 to 3 inches in length).

- When slicing or dicing hot chiles, always
- Always use disposable gloves when handling peppers, as their compounds can cause severe skin irritation.
- Do not brush your face, especially near your eyes.

Mild peppers include bell, sweet cherry, pimiento, and sweet banana and are typically larger (4 to 10 inches) than spicy peppers.

- When a recipe calls for long green chilies, a milder pepper may be substituted.
- It is possible that the skin of long green chilies is strong and can

be removed by heating the peppers.
- Peppers need not be peeled if they are coarsely chopped.

ONIONS

Onions that are red, yellow, white, and purple are interchangeable.

Corrosive substances

Adding acid to salsa is required for safe preservation.

Because the acidity of tomatoes varies considerably, additional acid must be added to make salsa safe.

- Commercially bottled lemon or lime juice or vinegar with a 5% acidity level are examples of commercially bottled citrus beverages. Lemon juice or vinegar with an acidity level of 5% is utilized.
- Lemon or lime juice is more acidic and has a smaller flavoring effect than vinegar.
- Follow the instructions in the recipe when adding vinegar or bottled lemon or lime juice to home-canned salsa.
- If not specified in the tested recipe, do not substitute vinegar for bottled lemon or lime juice, as this substitution may result in an unsafe product.

If you are not following a tested recipe or prefer to be inventive with your salsa mixtures, refrigerate them for up to a week or freeze them for up to a year. There are only salsa recipes and canning procedures that have been evaluated and approved by the USDA. There is no pressure-canning method for salsa that has been tested.

Fruit-Based Salsa Recipes

I've had a yearning for all kinds of fresh fruit as the weather has become increasingly warm. This fruit salsa recipe satisfies all your cravings, and it's also mildly savory, so it pairs well with so many different meals!

Many fruit salsa recipes resemble fruit salad and are served with cinnamon-sugar-sweetened crackers. I like the concept, but I believe fruit also tastes great when prepared with onion, garlic, lime juice, and salt. Until you've experienced it, you shouldn't criticize it.

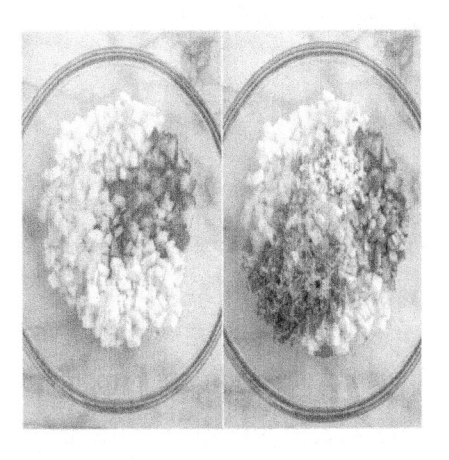

Fruit Salsa Recipe Ingredients

I used fresh, diced pineapple. If desired, tinned pineapple may be utilized.

Mango: I peeled and diced one mango of medium size after removing the seed. I frequently see pre-diced mango for sale in grocery stores, which would be a fantastic alternative.

Strawberry: Fresh strawberries enhance the flavor and color of this fruit salsa.

Jicama: Jicama is technically a root vegetable, not a fruit, but it has a nice crunch and a slightly sweet flavor, so I thought it would be a wonderful addition to this fruit salad. The pre-diced jicama I purchased from Trader Joe's worked wonderfully.

Red Onion: I utilized red onion because I adored the purple hue of this fruit salsa, but white onion would also work.

Two minced garlic bulbs were utilized. I would recommend fresh garlic rather than pre-diced garlic for this recipe.

Cilantro: Cilantro lends this fruit salsa a wonderfully fresh taste! If you don't like cilantro, you can substitute mint or coriander for it.

Lime Juice: I prefer to use freshly strained lime juice rather than the bottled variety, but either will suffice.

Salt: to flavor

How to Prepare the Finest Fruit Salsa

1. Start by dicing up all the ingredients. I like to dice everything into relatively small pieces so that the fruit salsa resembles pico de gallo. I dice the jalapeo smaller than the rest of the ingredients so that no one receives a large bite.

2. Mango, strawberries, pineapple, jicama, red onion, jalapeo, and garlic should be combined in a large basin. Then, incorporate a fistful of chopped cilantro, lime juice,

and salt. Combine all ingredients, test, and if necessary, add additional salt.

3. Refrigerate up to 4 days or consume immediately. Corn crackers are provided.

Sauce Recipes

Sauce recipes: What is a meatloaf without a flavorful brown sauce to accompany it, or a grilled satay without a lip-smacking peanut sauce to dip it in? Can you fathom biting into a chocolate tart or digging into a bowl of ice cream without a drizzle of salted caramel sauce? Sauces may not always be the focal point of a dish, but without them, many recipes would be incomplete, deficient in flavor, or unable to strike a chord.

While French cuisine reigns supreme when it comes to sauces, with classics such as Béchamel, Hollandaise, Veloute, and Espagnole, other cuisines, such as Asian, British, and Italian, also boast incredibly distinct sauce recipes that will leave you wanting more. The preparation of sauces may be simple, requiring only a few ingredients, but it is essential to achieve the proper flavor balance.

Before adding the liquid component, the majority of European sauce recipes begin with a roux, which requires cooking flour and butter in equal portions over medium heat. The roux thickens the sauce, allowing you to reduce it to the desired consistency, and provides a base to which you can add stock, dairy, tomatoes, and other flavoring ingredients.

Ingredients such as soy, oyster, peanuts, chili peppers, and others, along with thickening carbohydrates and jaggery, are utilized to create a wide variety of tantalizing Asian sauces. A good sauce is one that is viscous and not runny, smooth, adheres to the dish when poured on top, and has a flavor combination that is just right.

Whether you are cooking eggs in the morning, grilling a steak, or tossing vegetables, you can use a variety of sauces to enhance standard recipes. Are you unsure of how to begin? Fret not. To assist you in getting started, we have compiled a selection of our thirteen favorite sauce recipes from a variety of cuisines. Once you've mastered the fundamentals of a recipe, you're free to experiment with various flavor profiles.

Here are the top 13 homemade sauce recipes:

1. Asian Black Bean Sauce

In Asian cuisine, vermicelli and stir-fries are frequently served with black bean sauce. Black beans, peanuts, and rice wine are combined to create a flavorful marinade.

2. Cola BBQ Sauce

Unique barbecue marinade! This beverage has a strong cola flavor along with peppers, jalapeos, and Tabasco to increase the spiciness.

3. The sauce is salted caramel.

There's no better way to enhance your favorite confection than with a drizzle of salted caramel sauce. This recipe is simple and will leave your digits licking clean.

4. Peanut Sauce

Without this peanut marinade, chicken satays would be nearly insufficient. You may also serve it with chicken or vegetable kebabs. Click here for the recipe.

5. Sweet and Sour Sauce

This all-time favorite sauce is perfect for tossing vegetables, chicken, or fish to create a delicious dish. Add some chili flakes to increase the level of spiciness.

6. Tomato with Basil Sauce

This basic tomato and basil sauce with onions, chili flakes, balsamic vinegar, and black pepper drizzled over silky pasta is delectable.

7. Schezwan Sauce

A fiery Chinese condiment that pairs well with fried rice, noodles and even meat dishes.

8. Garlicky Tahini Sauce

This Middle Eastern classic marinade is simple to prepare. You can spread it on your shawarma or pair it with skewers.

9. Walnut Sauce

A delicious walnut sauce with sesame and garlic that can be served with crostini or raw vegetables.

10. White Sauce

This classic sauce is easy to prepare and, if done correctly, can transform a dish into a scrumptious delight.

11. Aubergine Chermoula Sauce Recipe

Chermoula is a marinade condiment used as a base for numerous Moroccan dishes. This version, comprised of eggplant, basil, dried herbs, and citrus, is an incredible dip.

12. Mexican Barbeque Sauce Recipe

Hot and spicy Mexican barbecue sauce that pairs well with nachos and other snacks. To prepare this delicious sauce, you only need olive oil, onion, garlic, chili pepper, tomatoes, beer, etc.

13. Bolognese Sauce Recipe

Bolognese sauce is an Italian meat sauce that is comprised of ground meat, grated onion, tomato purée, garlic paste, oregano, olive oil, etc. Prepare this special Italian sauce to enhance the flavor of your delicacies.

Relish Recipes

When you want to add some flavor to your meals, try these simple relish recipes. There is something delectable for everyone between the hot chiles and onions.

Relish is the ideal method to preserve the best flavors of the season, and you'll be able to enjoy them all year long.

1. Homemade Sweet Pickle Relish

Who doesn't adore pickles? With its crisp, briny flavor and juicy texture, it is the ideal accompaniment to any dish.

This sweet pickle relish enhances the flavor of pickles and has a shelf life of weeks.

In addition, it is comprised of delectable ingredients such as cucumbers, peppers, onions, and spices in a sour-sweet sauce.

2. Zucchini Relish

This zucchini relish recipe is my new obsession.

You can even add a spoonful to salads for an extra kick!

Combining sweet peppers and savory onions, this relish is tangy. What's the best? It is incredibly simple to prepare and imparts a crisp, refreshing taste to any dish.

3. Onion condiment

Are you sick of the same uninspired condiments at your spring and summer barbecues? If so, you're in for a treat!

This onion relish is an excellent alternative to pickle relish. It is slightly sweet, spicy, and sour, making it an excellent condiment for hot dogs and sausages.

Believe me, it's worth the extra effort.

4. Hot Pepper Mustard

Can't get enough of this hot and sweet pepper action?

I'm with you there. Fortunately, peppers are the star of this simple relish recipe.

This straightforward method is a fantastic way to preserve chili peppers for consumption throughout the year and can be applied to any variety.

Pepper relish is a condiment that can be used on nearly everything. From scrambled eggs to grilled cheese sandwiches, it will enhance each dish!

5. Spicy and Sweet Pickle Relish

I adore pickles, so it is only natural that I also enjoy pickle relish.

Despite its reputation as a condiment for hot dogs, it is so much more!

Try it on salads or add it to your charcuterie board. You can even use it as part of a seasoning blend to create a secret sauce!

6. The Southern Chow Chow

Forget about exotic ingredients and pricey spices; this relish is made with ordinary pantry staples.

Chow chow relish is a Southern staple that is ideal for adding a little kick to your dishes.

At any potluck, it will undoubtedly be devoured first.

This delicious combination of cabbage, onions, peppers, spices, and sauces will become a staple in your kitchen.

7. Dill Pickle Relish

This recipe for dill pickle relish is perfect for canning novices!

It's simple and straightforward, but you'll feel like a pro once you're finished.

Also, your friends and family will be impressed by its homemade deliciousness, so feel free to give these as gifts!

This relish has just enough heat to make it interesting, but not so much heat that it overpowers everything else on your plate.

CHAPTER 8

Introduction to Canning Meats and Soups

CANNING SOUP:

Due to the convenience of tinned soup, numerous food preservers would like to recreate soups from delis and supermarkets.

However, a home canner cannot safely replicate some delicacies that are commercially prepared. Creamed soups are not suitable for home canning because their constituents prevent the proper transfer of heat during processing, which can result in foodborne illness.

Freezing soups containing potentially hazardous ingredients is the preferable option. Penn State Extension has published Let's Preserve Soup, a thorough guide to preserving and freezing soup.

Ineffective Ingredients in Canned Soup

- Adding flour or other thickening agents to a product intended for home canning prevents heat from penetrating to the center of the jar, interfering with a secure process to eliminate botulism-causing bacterial spores.
- Never add thickening agents to homemade preserved goods during

processing. Add flour, cornmeal, or another thickening agent when the dish is ready to be served.
- The only exception to this rule is when a scientifically researched and tested recipe calls for Clear Jel®, such as in pie fillings or in small quantities in a few piquant recipes.
- Developing your own canning recipe is not secure.
- Butter, milk, cream, cheese, and other dairy products are low-acid foods that should never be added to soups before processing. Just prior to serving, add butter and milk to the chowder.

- Similarly, starch-rich substances impede thermal processing, avoid adding noodles, alphabet noodles, spaghetti, or any other type of pasta, rice, or barley to canned soups, serve canned soups or stews with noodles, any variety of pasta, rice, or dumplings.

Clearly Identifiable Soups
Let's Preserve: Soup

- Vegetable soups with a broth base can be reliably canned using the processing time required for the ingredient that requires the longest time to process individually.
- Depending on container size and soup ingredients, the majority

of soups will require 60 to 90 minutes to process in a pressure canner.
- Never preserve broth in half-gallon jars.
- Be careful not to load the jars with ingredients too tightly.
- Fill the jars halfway with solids, add broth, leaving a 1-inch headspace, and process in a pressure canner for vegetable soup. There must be room between the food particles for the hot liquid to percolate.
- The vegetables can be combined with cooked beef or poultry to produce a vegetable-meat soup.
- It is improper to can thickened or creamed tomato broth. Instead, use tomato juice, a tomato-vegetable juice combination, or crushed tomatoes (without vegetables). When you are ready to prepare the soup, open the jar of tomato product and add the desired vegetables, seasonings, and thickeners. Pouring the heated tomato mixture into a heated white sauce produces a delicious cream of tomato broth.
- Do not can soups made with pumpkin, winter squash, broccoli, or cauliflower, These ingredients impede safe processing and are packaged together, These broth recipes have not been subjected to scientific testing.
-

Freezing Soup

How do you safely store the stews listed above? Freeze it.

- Although freezing temperatures do not kill bacteria, they do not thrive in the freezer.
- Using a modified starch that is suitable for low temperatures such as ThermFlo® will prevent separation in thickened soups.
- Pumpkin, butternut squash, cauliflower, and broccoli soups that have been frozen retain their essence.
- Vegetable and meat dishes with pasta, rice, or noodles can be safely frozen. However, during stowage in the freezer, the starch in these products may soften.
- Remember to allow frozen soup sufficient time to defrost in the refrigerator; if defrosted in the microwave, the soup should be heated and consumed promptly.

Canning Meat and Poultry

Canning is a wonderful way to preserve and extend the shelf life of a variety of foods, including meat products. Using safe preparation and storage methods permits anyone to store nutrient-rich, high-quality protein. It is essential to exercise safe food handling, storage, and preparation techniques, as contaminated food will not be safe to consume after being canned.

Storage and preparation

MEATS

For meats such as beef, pork, venison, bear, lamb, or veal, cut the meat into strips, chunks, or parts that are sized appropriately for pint or quart jars, Leave approximately 1 inch of headspace at the top of the container when storing meat using either the hot pack or raw pack method.

Add a label and a date to your storage container, and then position it in a cool, dry, and dark location. After preparation, meat canned in jars should be consumed within 18 months.

Tips:

- To prevent off-flavors, remove visible fat from wild game.
- To reduce the intensity of the flavor of wild meats, age the carcasses at 40 degrees Fahrenheit or below for two to three days and marinate the harvested meat for one hour in brine water containing one tablespoon of salt per quart. Rinse well.
- When preserving leaner portions of meat, such as venison, the addition of animal fat, such as pork fat, aids in the preservation process and enhances the flavor of the final product. You can purchase pork fat for a nominal fee from your local butcher.

POULTRY

For meats such as poultry, duck, and goose, cut the meat

into strips, chunks, or pieces of the appropriate size for pint and quart jars. Leave approximately 1 inch of headspace at the top of the container when storing meat using either the hot pack or raw pack method.

Add a label and a date to your storage container, and then position it in a cool, dry, and dark location. After preparation, meat canned in jars should be consumed within 18 months.

Pressure Canning

It is essential to use the proper equipment when canning meats and poultry. Only a pressure canner can achieve the high temperature required to destroy harmful microbes in meat. Water bath canning methods, which are used to store high-acid or acidified foods, will not attain the necessary temperature and are therefore unsuitable for canning meat.

Canning Soups and Stews

Once you grasp the fundamentals of canning your own recipes, the pleasure of preserving foods for your family's consumption is extremely simple. Is it necessary? Indeed, it is the case.

I do not consider myself a renegade canner. There is a line that must be followed in order to combine scientific and conventional methods; one must merely be aware of this equilibrium.

There are some tips that follow will enable you to confidently and correctly can your favorite soups, stews, and other foods.

1. Preserving prepared or leftover foods

Can I can food? is the most frequently asked query. The brief answer is "yes," but why would you?

Meat and vegetables are the components of leftovers, both of which have been previously prepared. These foods will become undercooked if they are processed in a pressure canner a second time. The flesh will dry out, and the vegetables will become extremely mushy. Consequently, the cuisine is quite unappealing.

2. Uncooked or heated

Using the following two methods, soups and stews can be canned:

Raw pack: Place uncooked meat, vegetables, herbs, and seasonings in a hot jar containing hot liquid.

Packing heat

1. Prepare the meat by gently roasting, stewing, or browning it while keeping the center rare.

2. Remove the meat's bones and cut it into 1-inch segments.

3. Ensure that the meat, vegetables, and packaging liquid of choice are submerged in a stockpot containing the solids.

4. Add the desired seasonings and the appropriate quantity of ClearJel if a thicker consistency is desired. Refer to the container's instructions to determine how much to apply.

5. Bring the ingredients to a rolling boil and allow them to simmer for two minutes.

6. Remove the pan from the heat and transfer the solids into jars. Next, fill jars with a 1-inch headspace using a ladle.

Which procedure is superior? In actuality, it will depend on you. Obviously, hot-packing soups and stews impart more flavor than raw-packing, but raw-packing is equally tasty once herbs and seasonings are added.

3. Thickeners

Everyone enjoys ready-to-eat meals. The procedure for opening a jar of home-canned deer stew should be stew-like and viscous The healthiest and most delectable convenience foods.

There are ways to make a stew that is hearty, rich, and thick, but you must know which method is suitable for home preservation.

ClearJel is the only approved thickening agent for home-canned food. This product remains liquid throughout the canning procedure, allowing the heat to properly permeate the jar.

Why is this necessary? If the heat cannot reach the center of the container, any surviving botulism spores will be able to survive.

Not approved thickeners: The following thickeners are not approved, and here's why: Depending on the amount of thickener used, the contents of the jar may become too thick to enable proper heat penetration.

Remember that heat from the pressure canner must be able to reach the interior of the jars in order to kill any botulism spores.

- Flour
- Cornstarch
- Chia seeds
- The origin
- Tapioca

4. Cream and milk

Home-canned products containing milk or cream run the risk of becoming rancid, thereby deteriorating and resulting in waste. Milking is possible, but that does not make it proper. As a sustainable farm, we endeavor to eliminate waste, so even the possibility of milk or cream spoiling is considered wasteful.

5. Rice, Pasta, and Grains

Similar to thickeners, rice, pasta, and cereals should not be added to soups and stews that have been home-canned. These items may become exceptionally thick within the jar during the canning process, preventing heat from reaching the center of the jar.

It is best to can soups and stews without these ingredients and to add them just before serving.

6. Beans and peas

Beans and peas can be used in soups, stews, and chili, but they must be rehydrated before being canned. You have two options for preparing beans and peas for home-canned soup, both of which are quite simple:

- Ensure that the legumes are completely submerged in water while soaking them overnight.
- Two minutes after boiling, drain legumes or peas. Allow the peas to drain for approximately one hour to ensure that all the water has evaporated.

7. Meat and Vegetables

The pleasure of canning homemade soups and stews comes from using foods that your family will enjoy. Including the sort of meat utilized. You can choose from beef, poultry, pork, rabbit meat, and even wild game.

Having said that, you should be cognizant of the following:

- Items such as cabbage, Brussels sprouts, and spaghetti squash that do not retain their texture should not be canned. Stick with items that have a firm texture.
- Remove all bones and as much fat as possible from the canned flesh.

8. Seasonings and Herbs

The real pleasure of pressure-canning soups and stews is creating flavors that your family will enjoy. Salt is not required for home canning and should not be added, particularly if you are monitoring your sodium intake. Neither is rosemary if the flavor is not to your liking. Preserving homemade soups and stews is ideal for people with food allergies and dietary restrictions.

9. Liquid Base for Soups and Stews

The following liquids may comprise the contents of a jar:

- Water
- Broth
- Stock
- The liquids from whole tomatoes

Note: Soups and stews that are raw-packed gain flavor from the meat and seasonings that are added. However, heated packaging and the addition of water produce a more flavorful product.

Recipes for Canned Meats and Soups

1. Canned Chicken Noodle Soup:

Ingredients:

1 can of chicken noodle soup

1 cup of cooked chicken, shredded

1/2 cup of mixed vegetables (carrots, peas, corn)

Salt and pepper to taste

Instructions:

Step 1: Open the can of chicken noodle soup and pour it into a medium-sized saucepan.

Step 2: Place the saucepan on the stove over medium heat.

Step 3: Add the cooked chicken and mixed vegetables to the saucepan.

Step 4: Stir the soup occasionally and cook until it's heated through, about 5-7 minutes.

Step 5: Taste the soup and season with salt and pepper according to your preference.

Step 6: Once the soup is hot and the flavors have melded together, remove it from the heat.

Step 7: Serve the canned chicken noodle soup hot and enjoy!

2. Canned Tuna Salad:

Ingredients:

1 can of tuna, drained

1/4 cup mayonnaise

2 tablespoons diced celery

2 tablespoons diced red onion

1 tablespoon lemon juice

Salt and pepper to taste

Lettuce leaves (optional)

Bread or crackers for serving

Instructions:

Step 1: Open the can of tuna and drain the liquid.

Step 2: In a mixing bowl, combine the drained tuna, mayonnaise, diced celery, diced red onion, and lemon juice.

Step 3: Mix all the ingredients together until well combined.

Step 4: Season the tuna salad with salt and pepper according to your taste.

Step 5: If desired, line a serving plate with lettuce leaves.

Step 6: Scoop the tuna salad onto the lettuce leaves or serve it directly on bread or crackers.

Step 7: Serve the canned tuna salad chilled and enjoy!

3. Canned Beef Stew:

Ingredients:

1 can of beef stew

1/2 cup diced potatoes

1/2 cup diced carrots

1/4 cup frozen peas

1/4 cup frozen corn

Salt and pepper to taste

Instructions:

Step 1: Open the can of beef stew and pour it into a medium-sized saucepan.

Step 2: Place the saucepan on the stove over medium heat.

Step 3: Add the diced potatoes and carrots to the saucepan.

Step 4: Stir in the frozen peas and corn.

Step 5: Cook the stew, stirring occasionally, until the vegetables are tender, usually about 10-15 minutes.

Step 6: Taste the stew and season with salt and pepper according to your preference.

Step 7: Once the stew is heated through and the vegetables are cooked, remove it from the heat.

Step 8: Serve the canned beef stew hot and enjoy!

4. Canned Corned Beef Hash:

Ingredients:

1 can of corned beef hash

1 small onion, chopped

1 small bell pepper, chopped

2 cloves of garlic, minced

Salt and pepper to taste

Vegetable oil for frying

Fried eggs (optional, for serving)

Instructions:

Step 1: Heat a small amount of vegetable oil in a skillet over medium heat.

Step 2: Add the chopped onion, bell pepper, and minced garlic to the skillet. Sauté until the vegetables are softened.

Step 3: Open the can of corned beef hash and add it to the skillet with the sautéed vegetables.

Step 4: Break up the corned beef hash with a spoon and mix it with the vegetables.

Step 5: Cook the mixture, stirring occasionally, until the hash is heated through and slightly crispy, usually about 10-15 minutes.

Step 6: Taste the corned beef hash and season with salt and pepper according to your preference.

Step 7: If desired, serve the corned beef hash with fried eggs on top.

Step 8: Serve the canned corned beef hash hot and enjoy!

5. Canned Tomato Soup with Grilled Cheese Sandwich:

Ingredients:

1 can of tomato soup

1 cup of milk

Salt and pepper to taste

Sliced bread

Cheese slices

Butter

Instructions:

Step 1: Pour the can of tomato soup into a saucepan.

Step 2: Add milk to the saucepan and stir well to combine.

Step 3: Place the saucepan on the stove over medium heat and bring the soup to a simmer.

Step 4: Stir occasionally and cook the soup for about 5 minutes, until it's heated through.

Step 5: Taste the soup and season with salt and pepper according to your preference.

Step 6: While the soup is cooking, prepare the grilled cheese sandwich by placing cheese slices between two slices of bread.

Step 7: Butter the outsides of the bread slices.

Step 8: Heat a skillet or griddle over medium heat and place the sandwich on it.

Step 9: Cook the sandwich until the bread is golden brown and the cheese is melted, flipping it once.

Step 10: Remove the grilled cheese sandwich from the skillet and cut it into halves or quarters.

Step 11: Serve the canned tomato soup hot, alongside the grilled cheese sandwich.

Step 12: Dip the sandwich in the soup and enjoy!

6. Canned Clam Chowder

Ingredients:

1 can of clam chowder

1/2 cup diced potatoes

1/4 cup diced celery

1/4 cup diced onion

1/2 cup milk or heavy cream

Salt and pepper to taste

Fresh parsley (optional, for garnish)

Introduction:

Step 1: Open the can of clam chowder and pour it into a medium-sized saucepan.

Step 2: Place the saucepan on the stove over medium heat.

Step 3: Add the diced potatoes, celery, and onion to the saucepan.

Step 4: Stir in the milk or heavy cream, and bring the chowder to a gentle simmer.

Step 5: Cook the chowder, stirring occasionally, until the potatoes are tender, usually about 10-15 minutes.

Step 6: Taste the chowder and season with salt and pepper according to your preference.

Step 7: Once the chowder is heated through and the flavors have melded together remove it from the heat.

Step 8: If desired, garnish the clam chowder with fresh parsley for added freshness and color.

Step 9: Serve the canned clam chowder hot and enjoy!

7. Canned Minestrone Soup:

Ingredients:

1 can of minestrone soup

1/2 cup diced zucchini

1/2 cup diced carrots

1/4 cup diced celery

1/4 cup diced onion

1/2 cup cooked pasta (such as macaroni or shells)

Grated Parmesan cheese (optional, for serving)

Fresh basil or parsley (optional, for garnish)

Instructions:

Step 1: Open the can of minestrone soup and pour it into a medium-sized saucepan.

Step 2: Place the saucepan on the stove over medium heat.

Step 3: Add the diced zucchini, carrots, celery, and onion to the saucepan.

Step 4: Stir the soup and vegetables together, and bring it to a simmer.

Step 5: Cook the soup, stirring occasionally, until the vegetables are tender, usually about 10-15 minutes.

Step 6: Add the cooked pasta to the soup and stir to combine.

Step 7: Continue cooking the soup for a few more minutes until the pasta is heated through.

Step 8: Taste the minestrone soup and adjust the seasoning if necessary.

Step 9: If desired, serve the soup with a sprinkle of grated Parmesan cheese on top.

Step 10: Garnish with fresh basil or parsley for added flavor and presentation.

Step 11: Serve the canned minestrone soup hot and enjoy!

These recipes provide simple ways to enhance the flavors and textures of canned meats and soups by incorporating additional ingredients and seasonings. Feel free to modify them based on your preferences and dietary needs.

CHAPTER 9

Canning Fruits and Vegetables

If you're a cultivator, you've likely discovered that each season you have an abundance of produce that your family cannot possibly consume before it spoils. Have you ever attempted home canning? Canning fruits and vegetables can reduce food waste and supply the pantry with nutritious produce during the off-season.

Why Should Fruits and Vegetables Be Canned

Canning is a method of preserving fresh food in jars or other containers using heat and pressure. It eliminates hazardous microorganisms and preserves freshness. Because the food in Your can or jar will be entirely sterile, it will not perish until it is opened. Once a can is opened and no longer airtight airborne microorganisms can access your food. Because of this, you must "refrigerate the contents after opening."

Some produce may require a different preservation method than others.

The stages below outline fundamental canning guidelines for fruits and vegetables.

How to Can Friuts

The majority of fruit-canning recipes call for a straightforward syrup (a mixture of sugar and water) to preserve the fruit's flavor. Depending on the variety of fruit, you will use either a light or a thick syrup.

Step 1: Prepare fruit and canning jars.

Depending on the amount of produce you are canning, you will need a large number of Mason jars or similar containers of various sizes. Prepare your canning jars and collect the fruit you intend to preserve. Using soap and hot water, sterilize the jars and their closures.

Utilizing a dishwasher is the preferred method for sanitizing. Upon removal from the dishwasher, ensure that the canisters are not broken. Select and thoroughly rinse only the most recent produce available. Depending on the type of fruit being preserved, you may need to peel it. Peaches are among the fruits that can be "slipped." This simply entails removing the fruit's shell prior to canning. These fruits are dipped momentarily in boiling water until the skin splits.

Place them in cold water afterwards. The epidermis will simply flake away. Remember to remove any cavities, cores, or other portions that will not be consumed. Cut and prepare your produce using a cutting board.

Mix one cup of water with one-fourth to one-half cup of sugar for every quart of canned food. The type of syrup you prepare will depend on how sweet the fruit is and how "syrupy" you want it to be.

Step 2: Filling and sealing

Fill the canning jars with fruit, then use a funnel with a wide neck to add the syrup. By scraping along the sides of the filled jars with a knife, air pockets at the bottom of the jars can be removed. Leave a one-inch expansion space at the top of the container. Make sure the lids are secure but not overly rigid, and then screw them on.

Step 3: Start canning

Ensure that you adhere to the instructions included with your pressure canner. Place your canned produce in the canner and ensure that the water inside covers the jars halfway.

Lock the canner's lid and increase the heat to enable pressure to build within the device. Be sure to adhere to the manufacturer's instructions and keep a close eye on the pressure. Maintain the prescribed pressure for the specified period of time, typically 20 minutes. Use the stove's temperature controls to regulate the pressure.

Turn off the heat and allow the canner to settle once the process is complete. After the pressure gauge returns to zero, open the container. To remove the jars, use heavy-duty forceps or a jar lifter.

Let the vessels cool for approximately 24 hours. Then, by depressing the lids of the canisters, confirm that the appropriate seals have formed. If it returns after being depressed, the lid did not seal correctly. Be careful to refrigerate and consume the contents of any non-sealed jars within a few days, or freeze them for later use.

How to Can Vegetables

As with fruit, canning vegetables requires the addition of liquid. However, vegetable canning typically calls for a brine (water and salt) mixture. Check the NCHFP website for more information.

Step 1: Prepare vegetables and containers

As with fruit, you'll need a large quantity of canning jars or similar containers. Ideally, sterilize the jars and their covers by washing them with hot water and soap in the dishwasher. Ensure there are no cracks in the canisters.

Collect the vegetables intended for canning. Make sure they're as fresh as possible. As soon as you have inspected, selected, peeled, sliced, and washed garden-fresh vegetables, they should be canned. To prepare vegetables, use a cutting board. Remove the stems and any other unpalatable portions. Now is the time to add any preservatives if the particular canning recipe calls for them.

Step 2 is to fill and seal the jars.

Vegetables should be placed in the receptacles. Use a funnel with a wide mouth to transfer the brine into the containers, leaving an inch of headspace. By scraping along the sides of the filled jars with a knife, air pockets at the bottom of the jars can be removed. Screw on the lids, ensuring that they are secure and firm without being overtightened. Throughout the remainder of the canning procedure, air will continue to escape.

Step 3: Start canning

Fill the container of a large (20-quart) pressure canner with approximately 3 inches of water. Use a jar lifter or tongs to position your jars in the hot water inside the canner, To partially submerge the cans in water. As preparation steps can vary, be careful to adhere to the canner manufacturer's guidelines.

Securely fasten the canner's lid. Increase the heat to its maximum setting and allow steam to escape for approximately 10 minutes, then completely seal the canner and allow internal pressure to develop.

Ensure thorough monitoring of the pressure throughout the procedure. As the manufacturer has instructed, allow the pressure to rise to the appropriate level for canning. Once the required pressure has been attained, it must be maintained for the duration specified, typically 20 minutes. Use the stove's temperature controls to regulate the pressure.

After 20 minutes, or the time recommended by the manufacturer remove the canner from the heat and allow it to settle. When the pressure gauge reaches zero, allow steam to exit via the vent.

After the canner has cooled entirely, remove the jars using jar tongs and allow them to cool completely. This may take up to 24 hours. After the jars have chilled, examine their seals to ensure they are intact.

If the lid is indented and the center of the lid does not depress and spring back when pressed, the container has been properly sealed. If any of your jars did not seal properly, be sure to consume the vegetables from the non-sealed jars within a few days; handle them as you would fresh produce.

Canning Fruits: Techniques and Recipes

Canning fruits is a fantastic way to preserve their freshness and enjoy them throughout the year. This step-by-step guide will provide you with the necessary techniques and recipes to successfully can fruits at home. Whether you're a beginner or an experienced canner, these instructions will help you create delicious canned fruits that can be enjoyed for months to come.

Note: Before you begin, make sure to gather all the necessary equipment, including canning jars, lids, bands, a canning pot or large stockpot, a canning rack, a jar lifter, a funnel, a bubble remover, a ladle, and a clean kitchen towel.

1. Step 1: Selecting and Preparing Fruits

1. Choose fresh, ripe fruits that are in their prime. Select varieties that are suitable for canning, such as peaches, pears, apples, cherries, or berries.

2. Wash the fruits thoroughly under cold running water to remove any dirt or impurities.

3. Peel, pit, and slice the fruits as needed, following the specific instructions for each fruit. Remove any blemishes or damaged areas.

2. Step 2: Preparing the Canning Equipment

1. Inspect your canning jars for any cracks or chips. Discard any defective jars.

2. Wash the jars, lids, and bands in hot soapy water, rinse them well, and place them in a clean sink or large pot filled with hot water. Keep them warm until ready to use.

3. Fill the canning pot or large stockpot with enough water to

cover the jars by at least 1 inch. Place the canning rack inside the pot and heat the water to a simmer.

3. Step 3: Preparing the Syrup or Liquid

1. Determine the type of syrup or liquid suitable for the fruits you are canning. The options include light syrup, medium syrup, heavy syrup, fruit juice, or water.

2. Follow a trusted recipe or use the following guidelines to prepare the syrup:

- Light Syrup: Mix 2 1/4 cups of water with 1/2 cup of sugar.
- Medium Syrup: Mix 3 1/4 cups of water with 3/4 cup of sugar.
- Heavy Syrup: Mix 4 1/4 cups of water with 1 1/4 cups of sugar.

3. Heat the syrup or liquid in a saucepan until the sugar dissolves completely. Keep it warm until ready to use.

4. Step 4: Filling the Jars

1. Remove a jar from the hot water using the jar lifter, allowing the excess water to drain back into the pot.

2. Place the funnel on top of the jar and carefully pack the prepared fruit slices into the jar, leaving appropriate headspace as specified in your recipe (usually 1/2 to 1 inch).

3. Use the bubble remover or a non-metallic utensil to remove any air bubbles trapped inside the jar by gently pressing against the fruit slices.

4. Slowly pour the warm syrup or liquid into the jar, maintaining the specified headspace. Ensure that the fruit is fully covered by the liquid and there are no air pockets.

5. Wipe the jar's rim with a clean, damp kitchen towel to remove any fruit residue or syrup, ensuring a proper seal.

6. Place a lid on the jar, and screw the band on until it is fingertip tight. Do not over tighten.

5. Step 5: Processing the Jars

1. Using the jar lifter, carefully place the filled and sealed jar onto the canning rack in the pot of simmering water. Repeat this step for each jar, ensuring they are submerged in the water and spaced apart to allow for even heat distribution.

2. Once all the jars are in the pot, ensure that the water level is at least 1 inch above the jars. Add more hot water if necessary.

3. Increase the heat to bring the water to a rolling boil. Once boiling, start the processing time according to the specific fruit and recipe you are using. Refer to a trusted canning guide or recipe for the correct processing time.

4. Maintain a steady boil throughout the processing time, adjusting the heat as needed to prevent the water from boiling over.

5. When the processing time is complete, turn off the heat and carefully remove the jars using the jar lifter. Place them on a towel-lined countertop or cooling rack, leaving some space between the jars to cool.

6. Allow the jars to cool undisturbed for 12 to 24 hours. You may hear popping sounds as the lids seal.

7. After cooling, check the lids for proper sealing. Press the center of each lid to ensure it does not flex or pop back. If a lid does not seal, refrigerate the jar and consume its contents within a few days.

8. Remove the bands from the sealed jars and wipe them clean with a damp cloth. Label the jars with the contents and date.

9. Store the sealed jars in a cool, dark, and dry place. Canned fruits can generally be stored for up to 12 to 18 months. For optimal quality, consume them within the first year.

6. Step 6: Enjoying Your Canned Fruits

1. When you're ready to enjoy your canned fruits, remove the band from the jar and check the lid seal. If the lid is still tightly sealed and the fruit looks and smells good, it is safe to consume.

2. If the seal is intact but the fruit appears discolored, mushy, or has an off-putting odor, discard the contents as it may have spoiled.

3. Gently wash the jar to remove any residue before opening it.

4. Use a jar opener or your hands to carefully break the seal by prying the lid upward. Be cautious of any pressure that may have built up inside the jar during processing.

5. Pour the contents into a serving dish or use the fruit directly in recipes and desserts.

6. Canned fruits can be enjoyed on their own, used as toppings for yogurt or ice cream, incorporated into pies, cakes, and cobblers, or added to smoothies and fruit salads.

7. Step 7: Exploring Variations and Recipes

1. Experiment with different fruit combinations and flavors to create your own unique canned fruit recipes.

2. Explore recipes that incorporate spices like cinnamon, cloves, or vanilla for added flavor.

3. Consider canning fruits in fruit juices or syrups infused with herbs like mint or basil for a refreshing twist.

4. Look for trusted canning cookbooks or online resources for a wide range of tested fruit canning recipes.

5. Preserve seasonal fruits when they are at their peak to enjoy their flavors year-round.

8. Step 8: Maintaining Quality and Safety

1. Store opened jars of canned fruits in the refrigerator and consume them within a few days.

2. Always check for signs of spoilage before consuming canned fruits. If the lid is bulging, the contents have an off odor, or there are visible signs of mold or fermentation, discard the contents.

3. Do not consume canned fruits that show signs of leakage or have a broken seal.

4. Regularly inspect your canned fruits for any signs of spoilage or deterioration during storage. If in doubt, err on the side of caution and discard the contents.

5. Follow proper canning techniques and safety guidelines to ensure the long-term quality and safety of your canned fruits.

9. Step 9: Cleaning and Storing Canning Equipment

1. After you have finished canning your fruits, it's essential to clean and store your canning equipment properly for future use.

2. Wash the jars, lids, bands, and canning tools in hot soapy

water, ensuring that all residue is removed.

3. Rinse the equipment thoroughly with hot water to remove any soap residue.

4. Inspect the jars, lids, and bands for any signs of damage or wear. Discard any damaged or rusted components.

5. Dry the jars, lids, and bands completely before storing them to prevent the growth of mold or mildew.

6. Store the jars, lids, and bands in a clean and dry area away from direct sunlight and moisture.

7. Consider storing the jars with the bands off to prevent them from rusting or sticking to the lids.

8. Label any reusable lids with the date of purchase to keep track of their age and ensure they are used within a reasonable timeframe.

Step 10: Expanding Your Canning Skills

1. Canning fruits is just the beginning of your canning journey. Explore other canning techniques, such as canning vegetables, jams, jellies, and pickles.

2. Learn about safe canning practices, including proper pH levels, processing times, and adjustments for high-altitude canning.

3. Join canning communities or local canning groups to share tips, recipes, and experiences with fellow canning enthusiasts.

4. Attend canning workshops or classes to refine your skills and learn new techniques from experienced canners.

5. Continue to educate yourself on the latest research and guidelines for sa

Additional More Tips:

- Always follow tested canning recipes to ensure food safety.
- Adjust processing times based on your altitude if necessary. Higher altitudes may require longer processing times.
- Use proper canning techniques to prevent contamination and spoilage.

- If you're a beginner, consider taking a canning class or consulting a canning expert for additional guidance.

Now you're ready to enjoy the delicious flavors of canned fruits that will brighten up your meals and snacks throughout the year.

Remember, practice makes perfect, and the more you can, the more confident and skilled you'll become in preserving the flavors of your favorite fruits and expanding your culinary repertoire.

Canning Vegetables: Techniques and Recipes

Canning vegetables is a fantastic way to preserve the bounty of your garden or take advantage of seasonal produce. This step-by-step guide will walk you through the process of canning vegetables, providing you with techniques and recipes to ensure successful and safe preservation. Let's get started!

Step 1: Gather the Necessary Equipment

To begin canning vegetables, gather the following equipment:

- Large canning pot with a rack
- Canning jars with lids and bands
- Jar lifter
- Canning funnel
- Magnetic lid lifter
- Bubble remover and headspace tool
- Clean towels and cloths
- Cutting board and knife
- Vegetable peeler
- Non-reactive pot for blanching
- Label and Store

Step 2: Prepare Your Vegetables

Choose fresh and high-quality vegetables for canning. Wash them thoroughly and trim off any damaged or bruised parts. Depending on the vegetable, you may need to peel, core, or chop them into suitable sizes for canning.

Step 3: Prepare the Canning Jars

Wash the canning jars, lids, and bands with hot, soapy water. Rinse them well and place the jars in the canning pot filled with water. Bring the water to a simmer, but do not boil the jars at this point. Keep the lids and bands in a separate saucepan of hot water.

Step 4: Blanch the Vegetables

Blanching helps retain the flavor, color, and texture of the vegetables. Bring a pot of water to a boil and blanch the vegetables for a specific time (varies depending on the vegetable) until they are partially cooked. Immediately transfer them to an ice water bath to halt the cooking process. Drain the vegetables thoroughly.

Step 5: Fill the Jars

Using a canning funnel, carefully pack the blanched vegetables into the jars, leaving the recommended headspace (usually 1/2 to 1 inch) at the top. Use a bubble remover to eliminate any air bubbles by sliding it along the inside edge of the jar. Adjust the headspace if necessary.

Step 6: Add Liquid and Wipe the Jar Rims

Depending on the recipe and vegetable, add the appropriate liquid such as water, vegetable broth, or brine to cover the vegetables. Use the bubble remover to remove any additional bubbles. Wipe the rims of the jars with a clean, damp cloth to ensure a proper seal.

Step 7: Apply Lids and Bands

Using a magnetic lid lifter, remove a lid from the hot water and place it on the jar. Screw on the band until it is fingertip tight. Repeat this process for all the jars.

Step 8: Process the Jars

Using a jar lifter, carefully place the filled jars onto the rack in the canning pot. Ensure the jars are submerged in at least 1 inch of water. Bring the water to a full rolling boil and start the processing time according to the specific recipe. Adjust the processing time based on your altitude (refer to a reliable canning guide for adjustments).

Step 9: Remove Jars and Cool

After the processing time is complete, turn off the heat and allow the jars to sit in the pot for 5 minutes. Using a jar lifter, remove the jars from the pot and place them on a clean towel or cooling rack, leaving space between the jars. Avoid tilting or touching the lids at this stage.

Step 10: Check Seals and Store

As the jars cool, you will hear a popping sound, indicating a successful seal. After 12 to 24 hours, press down on the center of each lid to check for a proper seal. If the lid is firm and does not flex or pop back, the jar is sealed correctly. Any unsealed jars should be refrigerated and consumed within a few days.

Step 11: Label and Store

Once you have confirmed that all the jars are properly sealed, label each jar with the contents and the date of canning. Store the jars in a cool, dark place, such as a pantry or cellar, where they will be protected from direct sunlight and extreme temperature fluctuations. Canned vegetables can typically be stored for up to one year, but it's recommended to consume them within 6 to 8 months for the best quality.

Step 12: Enjoy Your Canned Vegetables!

Now that you have successfully canned your vegetables, it's time to enjoy the fruits of your labor. Canned vegetables can be used in a variety of recipes, from soups and stews to side dishes and salads. Remember to inspect each jar before use and discard any that show signs of spoilage, such as bulging lids, off odors, or visible mold.

Important Tips and Safety Precautions:

a. Always follow a trusted and up-to-date canning recipe from a reliable source.

b. Use proper canning techniques to ensure food safety and prevent the growth of harmful bacteria.

c. Adjust processing times according to your altitude for safe canning.

d. Use fresh and high-quality vegetables for the best results.

e. Inspect jars for signs of spoilage before consumption.

f. If in doubt about the safety of a jar or its contents, it's better to err on the side of caution and discard it.

Remember, canning vegetables is a rewarding and practical skill that allows you to enjoy the flavors of the season all year round. With proper techniques and careful attention to safety, you can confidently preserve your favorite vegetables and savor their taste long after they're out of season.

CHAPTER 10

Storing and Using Canned Goods

Canning is a fantastic method for preserving the freshness and flavors of seasonal fruits, vegetables, and other food items. Once you've mastered the art of canning, it's important to understand how to properly store and utilize your canned goods. This comprehensive guide will walk you through the best practices for storing canned goods and provide creative ideas for incorporating them into your meals.

Section 1: Storing Canned Goods

Choosing the Right Storage Space:

- Find a cool, dark, and dry area for storing canned goods.//
- Avoid areas exposed to direct sunlight, excessive heat, or extreme temperature fluctuations.
- Basements, pantries, or dedicated storage shelves are ideal.

Properly Labeling:

- Label each can with the contents and the date of canning.
- Use waterproof and smudge-resistant labels.
- Place older cans in front to ensure they are used first.

Organizing and Rotating:

- Arrange canned goods in a systematic manner.

- Group similar items together (e.g., fruits, vegetables, soups).

- Implement a "first in, first out" rotation system to use older cans before newer ones.

Checking for Spoilage:

- Regularly inspect canned goods for signs of spoilage, such as bulging lids, rust, leakage, or strange odors.

- Discard any cans that show signs of spoilage.

Section 2: Using Canned Goods

Food Safety Precautions:

- Always inspect cans before opening them.

- Wash hands thoroughly before handling canned goods.

- Use clean utensils to prevent cross-contamination.

Recipes and Meal Planning:

- Canned goods can be utilized in various recipes, including soups, stews, sauces, salads, and more.

- Get creative and experiment with different flavor combinations.

- Plan meals ahead of time to incorporate canned goods efficiently.

Enhancing Flavor and Nutrition:

- Combine canned ingredients with fresh herbs, spices, and other seasonings for added taste.

- Consider pairing canned fruits and vegetables with fresh produce for a nutritious and balanced meal.

Shelf Life and Expiration Dates:
- Canned goods generally have a long shelf life, ranging from one to five years.

- Check expiration dates and prioritize using older cans first.

- Although most canned goods remain safe to consume beyond their expiration dates, quality and flavor might degrade over time.

Donation and Sharing:

- If you have an excess of canned goods or won't be able to use them before their expiration dates, consider donating to local food banks or shelters.

- Share your homemade canned goods with friends, family, or neighbors to spread the joy of preserved flavors.

Storing and using canned goods effectively is essential for getting the most out of your preserved harvest. By following the proper storage guidelines, organizing your canned goods, and creatively incorporating them into your meals, you can enjoy the delicious flavors and nutritional benefits of your canned goods for an extended period. With these tips in mind, you'll be able to make the most of your canned treasures and savor the taste of the seasons all year round.

Factors that reduce the longevity of preserved foods.

Preserving food is a common practice to extend its shelf life and prevent spoilage. However, there are several factors that can reduce the longevity of preserved foods. Understanding these factors is crucial for maintaining food safety and quality. Here's a comprehensive guide on the factors that can affect the longevity of preserved foods:

1. Temperature:

The temperature at which preserved foods are stored plays a vital role in their longevity. Most preserved foods should be stored at a cool temperature to slow down the growth of bacteria and other microorganisms. Higher temperatures can accelerate spoilage and reduce the shelf life of preserved foods. It is important to store preserved foods in refrigerators or cool, dry areas away from direct sunlight or heat sources.

2. Moisture:

Moisture content is another critical factor that affects the longevity of preserved foods. Excess moisture can promote the growth of bacteria, molds, and yeasts, leading to spoilage. Preserved foods should be stored in dry conditions or with moisture-absorbing agents such as silica gel packets to maintain their quality and extend their shelf life.

3. Oxygen:

Oxygen can cause oxidative reactions that lead to the deterioration of preserved foods. Exposure to oxygen can cause rancidity in fats and oils, discoloration in fruits and vegetables, and loss of nutritional value. Vacuum-sealing, using airtight containers, or employing oxygen absorbers can help minimize the presence of oxygen and extend the shelf life of preserved foods.

4. pH Levels:

The acidity or alkalinity of preserved foods can influence their longevity. Low pH (acidic) foods, such as pickles or sauerkraut, have a longer shelf life compared to high pH (alkaline) foods. Acidic conditions create an inhospitable environment for bacterial growth. If you're preserving high pH foods, it's important to follow proper canning procedures to prevent the growth of harmful microorganisms.

5. Salt and Sugar:

Salt and sugar are commonly used in preserving foods due to their ability to draw out moisture, inhibit microbial growth, and enhance flavor. However, excessive or insufficient amounts of salt or sugar can negatively impact food preservation. It is important to follow recipes and guidelines for salt and sugar concentrations to ensure effective preservation and proper taste.

6. **Contamination:**

Contamination by microorganisms or other contaminants can significantly reduce the shelf life of preserved foods. It is crucial to practice proper hygiene during the preparation, handling, and packaging of preserved foods. Ensure that all utensils, containers, and equipment used are clean and sanitized. Additionally, using spoiled or damaged ingredients can introduce spoilage microorganisms into preserved foods, so it's essential to start with fresh and high-quality ingredients.

7. **Packaging:**

The choice of packaging material can affect the longevity of preserved foods. Proper packaging helps protect preserved foods from light, air, moisture, and microbial contamination. Depending on the type of preserved food, suitable packaging options may include glass jars, cans, vacuum-sealed bags, or airtight containers. It's important to select packaging that provides an effective barrier and maintains the quality of the preserved food.

8. **Quality of Ingredients:**

The quality of ingredients used in preserved foods can impact their longevity. Using fresh, ripe, and unspoiled ingredients will help ensure the preservation process starts with the best possible conditions. Inspect ingredients for any signs of damage or spoilage before preserving them.

9. **Preservation Method:**

Different preservation methods have varying effects on the longevity of preserved foods. Common preservation techniques include canning, freezing, drying, fermenting, and smoking. Each method has its own requirements and limitations. It's crucial to follow the recommended procedures for the chosen

10. **Time:**

Regardless of the preservation method employed, all preserved foods have a limited shelf life. Over time, even with proper storage and preservation techniques, the quality and nutritional value of preserved foods can deteriorate. It's important to label preserved foods with the date of preservation and consume them within the recommended time frame for optimal taste and safety.

11. Handling and Storage:
Improper handling and storage practices can also reduce the longevity of preserved foods. For example, exposing preserved foods to frequent temperature fluctuations, opening and closing containers excessively, or using dirty utensils can introduce contaminants and compromise the quality of the preserved food. It's important to handle and store preserved foods with care, following proper hygiene practices and avoiding unnecessary exposure to external elements.

12. Pest Infestation: Pest infestation, such as insects or rodents, can cause significant damage to preserved foods. They can contaminate the food, cause spoilage, and reduce its shelf life. Proper storage practices, such as using tightly sealed containers and regular inspection for signs of pest activity, can help prevent infestations and maintain the longevity of preserved foods.

13. Light Exposure: Light, especially sunlight, can accelerate the degradation of certain nutrients and cause color changes in preserved foods. UV radiation can also promote the growth of microorganisms. It is recommended to store preserved foods in dark or opaque containers and in areas away from direct light exposure.

14. Quality of Water:

Water quality used during the preservation process can affect the longevity of preserved foods. Contaminated water can introduce harmful microorganisms or impurities that compromise the safety and shelf life of preserved foods. It is essential to use clean, potable water for preserving foods and adhere to recommended guidelines for water quality in preservation recipes.

15. Over processing:

Overprocessing preserved foods, such as excessive heating or prolonged exposure to high temperatures, can result in loss of texture, flavor, and nutritional value. It's important to follow the recommended processing times and temperatures for specific preservation methods to ensure that the preserved foods retain their quality and longevity.

16. Quality of Seals:

If using canning or vacuum-sealing methods, the quality of seals plays a critical role in preserving the longevity of foods. Inadequate sealing can lead to air and moisture penetration, which can promote spoilage. It's important to check the seals regularly for any signs of leakage or damage and reseal or replace as necessary.

17. Specific Food Characteristics:

Different types of foods have varying characteristics that can impact their shelf life. Some foods, like fruits and vegetables, have higher water content and are prone to spoilage. Acidic foods tend to have a longer shelf life due to their inhospitable environment for microorganisms. Understanding the specific characteristics of the food being preserved is essential for applying appropriate preservation techniques and determining its expected shelf life.

By considering these factors and implementing proper preservation techniques, you can extend the longevity of preserved foods while maintaining their quality, safety, and nutritional value. Always refer to reliable preservation guidelines, recipes, and food safety recommendations for specific food items and methods to ensure the best results.

Shelf life and best practices for storage

The shelf life of food products refers to the length of time that a food product can be stored under specific conditions while maintaining its quality, freshness, and safety

Understanding Factors Affecting the Shelf Life of Food Products

All food has a shelf life, whether it's fresh, perishable,

or non-perishable. Every food product will have an expiry date that varies depending on the ingredients and the processing methods used.

We will explain the differences between high-risk and low-risk food groups, as well how each different processing method affects the longevity of the food. This article will also provide an overview of how to determine and increase shelf life of a product.

What is Food Shelf Life?

Shelf life is the time after production that the food remains safe to eat or the period food can be used while maintaining its quality.

Tip: It is an offence to sell goods past their use by date as they may not be safe for consumption.

High-risk Foods

High-risk foods are ready-to-eat foods and often contain the ideal conditions for bacterial growth such as moisture and a high protein content. These foods are often stored under refrigeration and are marked with a 'use-by' date. 'Use by' dates are used to indicate that a food could become harmful after that date. These dates are determined and verified through microbial testing.

Examples of high-risk foods include:

1. Cooked meat and poultry.

2. Smoked salmon.

3. Prepared salads and vegetables.

4. Dairy products, such as milk, cream and cheese.

5. Meat gravies, sauces, pâté and meat pies.

6. Foods made with uncooked egg, such as mousse and mayonnaise.

7. Seafood, such as cooked shellfish, prawns and oysters.

8. Cooked rice and pasta.

Frozen meat products and fish must show the date of freezing or the date of first freezing, if frozen more than once. Frozen meats going on to further processing must carry both the date of production and the date of freezing. The date on batches must be for the oldest component. Freezing makes the pathogens dormant and does not kill them. This is why it is not recommended to refreeze products, and mishandling a frozen product will affect the shelf life.

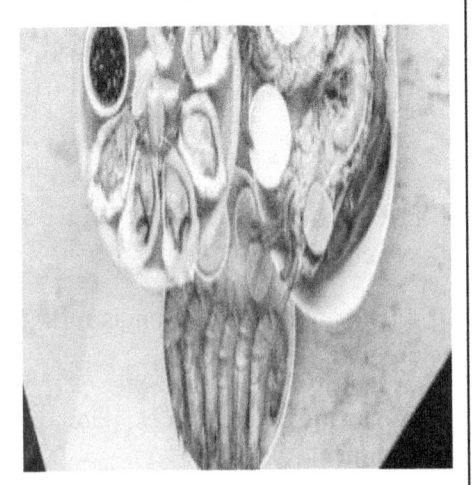

Low-risk Foods

Low-risk foods are often stable at ambient temperatures due to preservation methods such as dehydration or acid fermentation. These foods have a 'best before' date.

'Best before' dates apply to foods which will deteriorate in quality after the specified date, but which would not become harmful to health. These dates are determined by quality testing

Examples of low-risk foods include:

- Sweets.
- Pickles.
- Honey.
- Jam and preserves.
- Syrups.
- Vinegar.
- Flour and dried pasta.

The exemptions from date marking include drinks over 10% alcohol, sugar, salt, and products that are generally expected to be eaten on the day of purchase such as fresh fruit & vegetables and bakery products. 'Sell by', 'display until' and similar indications are retailer marks and have no legal significance.

It is important for all food manufacturers to have a good understanding of what makes a food high-risk or low-risk as it is one of the biggest factors that affect the shelf life of a product.

What are the Factors Affecting Shelf Life?

There are many factors that can affect the shelf life of different foods. It is important to know what these consist of – particularly for those who work in food manufacturing.

Intrinsic and Extrinsic Factors

Intrinsic factors are inherent within the food and cannot be controlled, such as:

- Water activity.
- Moisture content.
- pH.
- Salt content.
- Sugar content.
- Nutrient content.
- Oxidation potential.

Extrinsic factors are the shelf-life factors which can be controlled or changed, for example:

- Time.
- Temperature
- Modified Atmospheric Packaging (MAP) and packaging materials.
- Processing methods.
- Chemical preservatives.

Processing Methods

Processing methods are often used to kill bacteria and make the product uninhabitable for pathogens. For example:

1. Acid fermentation, such as kimchi.

2. Curing and smoking, such as cured meats and smoked salmon.

3. Thermal processes, such as UHT milk or juice pasteurisation within the packaging to ensure a long shelf life.

Product Formulation

The product formulation is one of the biggest factors that affect the shelf life. The 'clean label' and 'healthier' consumer demands pose a challenge to product developers. Sugar, salt and additives all contribute greatly to the shelf life of a product. Therefore, it isn't as simple as just reducing or removing them as consumers often expect the product attributes to stay the same.

Product Formulation: Water Activity

Water activity is a measure of available water, which is used to determine the potential growth of microorganisms. Each pathogen will have a different minimum level of water activity to allow growth. The measurement ranges from 0.0 to 1.0. For reference, pure water has a water activity measure of 1.0, fresh fruit, vegetables and meat all have a water activity measure of over 0.9, and biscuits are around 0.3.

A product with a water activity level below 0.8 reduces the number of microorganisms which are likely to grow to some moulds and yeasts. Jam, for example, has a high moisture content but is relatively low water activity measure (around 0.75 – 0.8). This is because the sugar binds to the water, making it unavailable for microbial growth. Salt has the same ability to bind to water as sugar, which is why it is challenging to reduce salt and sugar when reformulating a healthier product, especially if preservatives are also not used.

Product Formulation: Additives

Additives, such as preservatives and acidity regulators, can be used to increase the shelf life of a product. The pH is a measure of the acidity or alkalinity of something. Most often in food and drink products, an acidity regulator, such as citric acid, is used to ensure the product has a consistently low (acidic) pH as most bacteria prefer a neutral pH around 6.5 – 7.0.

Preservatives, such as sulphites, are also frequently used in long life products such as wine and dried fruits. The 'clean label' trend has driven the reformulation of many supermarket products with claims such as 'no nasties' and 'no artificial preservatives' now expected from consumers. The demand for fewer allergens also affects sulphite containing products because sulphites are one of the 14 named allergens.

Products aiming to comply with 'clean label' ideals are more difficult to formulate to have the same shelf life as their high sugar, salt and preservative-containing competitors.

Food products often have a 'rework' recipe version if there is leftover or safe rejected product (such as not meeting the correct weight) from a previous production run. Adding rework at high quantities may affect the structure and quality of certain products.

Recipes which include rework should be sensory tested to find out if there is a difference in taste and texture, compared to a recipe without rework. Sensory testing will also allow you to find the percentage of rework that can be added without altering the shelf life of the product. For example, adding reworked set fudge to a fudge mixture will reduce waste but may affect the texture and quality shelf life of the fudge.

Packaging

Packaging can be used to extend the shelf life of products, examples include:

- Modified Atmospheric Packaging, such as adding carbon dioxide to ready-to-eat ham slices.
- Vacuum packing, for example, when steaks are vacuum packed to remove oxygen from the packaging.
- Sealed plastic, such as the plastic packaging in cereal boxes, to prevent the cereal from going soft.
- Canning.

The type of packaging material used greatly influences the shelf life of products.

Storage and Transportation

Times, temperatures and conditions all play a major role in maintaining the shelf life of a product. A product will have a specification which will contain the temperatures and conditions the product should be stored and shipped. For example, ambient 'stored in a cool and dry place', frozen or chilled 'this product must be kept refrigerated'. If the storage and transportation of a product is not safe or falls outside of the product specifications, the product can spoil faster than its declared shelf life.

During the movement of product – either from storage to the transport vehicle or from the transport vehicle to the retailer or distribution centre – products must maintain their specified conditions. If the temperature of a chilled product goes within the temperature danger zone, it could reduce the shelf life of the product and make the product unsafe. Equally, a frozen product must remain frozen otherwise the dormant microorganisms could continue to grow if the conditions become favourable again.

It is out of the hands of the manufacturer and retailer as to how a customer handles their products after purchase. For this reason, it is important to clearly state the storage instructions on the pack, as well as how long the product is safe after opening – for those products which quickly spoil once opened.

How to Determine the Shelf Life of Food Products

It is important to do your own testing to determine the shelf life of your products to verify that your products are safe to be consumed within the time period you specify. For longer life ambient-stable products, you want to set a shelf life where the quality of your product nearing the end of the shelf life is a product your customers will still be happy with.

How to Calculate Shelf Life

For perishable products, a microbial analysis is essential in determining and validating your 'use by' date. If you don't know where to start, take a look at industry publications and any potential legislation which may apply to your product. For example, in the UK, the maximum shelf life for meat products is 13 days, which was recently extended from 10.

For non-perishable ambient-stable products, microbial and sensory testing is often used in combination to determine the 'best before' date.

It is beneficial to gather as many measures as possible about your product. For example, the pH value, water activity, sugar content, salt content, alcohol content, viscosity, colour, total acidity (TA). This way you can adjust your recipe and measure more accurately to understand the compositional factors at play. The compositional profile can then be used as quality testing tolerances to ensure consistency and safety during manufacturing.

How to Increase the Shelf Life of Food Products

Each of these above factors play a role in the expiration of each food or drink product, whether it is microbial, or will impact on product quality. Multiple approaches to extending shelf life and food safety are used in the food industry. For example:

- Beer production uses alcohol, a low pH and pasteurisation to ensure a long shelf life.
- Jam production uses a high sugar content, acidity regulators and pasteurisation to reduce food spoilage.

The acidity measure is of far more importance when formulating a 'no added sugar' jam or 'low alcohol' beer.

Methods for Increasing Shelf Life

Research into novel packaging is one of the developments in how to determine shelf life. For example, Australian scientists have been researching visual indicators on packaging to indicate when foods are spoiled, in an attempt to reduce food waste.

You won't need to alter your product if you look into changing the packaging first. The different barrier qualities of each packaging type impact the shelf life of a product and help prevent it from spoilage or a reduction in quality which, in turn, reduces food waste going to landfill. For fresh products, MAP (Modified Atmospheric Packaging) greatly reduces spoilage.

If you are considering changing the formulation of your product, you must first consider your brand and company values. Do you aim to have 'no added sugar', 'no artificials' or 'no nasties' claims? If so, what healthier and natural ways can you reformulate to make it more difficult for microbial growth?

More consumer friendly ingredients include:

- Citric acid.
- Lemon juice.
- Antioxidants, such as rosemary extract, vitamin C or vitamin E.
- Vinegar.

Benefits of Extending Shelf Life

Benefits of extending the shelf life of foods include:

- A better quality product.
- Fewer shipments rejected.
- Less food loss and waste.
- Increased profit margins.
- Better brand reputation.

Whilst there are many factors which can affect the shelf life of all food products, it is important to understand what these are, how to determine the expiration of your products, and familiarise yourself with common methods used to extend the shelf life.

Factors that reduce the longevity of preserved foods.

Food storage is a good habit to develop for several reasons. These advantages range from cost savings to eating a healthy diet year-round. Above all, understanding how to maximize your food storage can promote relaxation and anxiety-free living.

Food storage is a fundamental home skill that has been utilized for thousands of years to prepare for famines and other times when food is scarce. After 4000 years, wheat preserved in Egyptian tombs in containers was still edible.

In an effort for families to be self-sufficient, food is regularly preserved and kept to be consumed from harvest to harvest. It's noteworthy to notice that practically all human societies and many animal species stockpile food. By keeping food on hand, you can frequently save time and money while also ensuring your safety and security.

There are numerous key reasons to store food:

- Food that has been gathered and processed is preserved for future use.
- All year long provides a healthy diet.
- Getting ready for disasters, emergencies, and food shortages
- Shortages or famine
- For religious grounds
- Mental calm
- Sustaining oneself

Food storage-related variables

TEMPERATURE: An important factor in food shelf life is the storage temperature. According to the United States Department of Agriculture, or USDA, the shelf life of stored food is halved for every 10.8 degree increase in temperature. A steady temperature between 40 and 60 degrees is the ideal range for food storage. Stay away from the cold.

MOISTURE: It is advised to eliminate moisture before storing food. Foods should have a moisture content of 10% or less when being stored for a long time.

OXYGEN: Foods store best when they are oxygen-free. Food molecules won't oxidize if oxygen is removed. In order to eliminate oxygen,

- Displace oxygen by purging the product's air with an inert gas (such as nitrogen). Utilized frequently is carbon dioxide gas, which dry ice releases and takes the place of oxygen.
- Air is primarily composed of two gases: nitrogen, which makes up about 78% of the volume, and oxygen, which makes up about 21%. If the oxygen is taken up, only 99% pure nitrogen in a partial vacuum is left.

LIGHT: Light is a type of energy that can make food less nutritious. Keep food in dimly lit spaces.

CONTAINER: Store food in containers made of food-grade plastic, metal, or glass to ensure that no substances that could contaminate and harm your health are present. Use airtight (hermetic)-sealed containers for the longest possible storage life. Air-tight containers include:

- 10 cans
- Sealable buckets for storing food
- Metal (lined) or plastic drums with seals are food-grade.
- Foil satchels
- Pete containers (for dry goods like beans, grains, and wheat)

The containers mentioned above, when combined with oxygen absorber packets, help maintain the nutritional value and flavor of food while also eradicating food-borne insects.

WARNING: If moist items are kept in oxygen-depleted packaging, botulism poisoning may occur. Products must be dry (have a moisture content of no more than 10%) in order to be stored in airtight containers with oxygen absorbers.

Dried foods kept at home are infested by a number of common insects. Put contaminated things in a deep freeze (zero degrees) for three to four days in order to control the problem using cold therapy. This will destroy any living insects, larvae, and eggs.

The "best if used by" date is the shelf date, which indicates that the majority of the flavor and nutrition are still present. The term "life-sustaining shelf life" refers to the amount of time that food is still safe to eat.

Understanding Factors Affecting the Shelf Life of Food Products

From cost savings to fewer meals wasted throughout the year, the practice of food storage is immensely advantageous.

For more than a thousand years, people have been storing food. Can you believe wheat found in Egyptian tombs kept in jars was still edible after 4,000 years?

If you are a restaurant owner and need assistance designing your commercial kitchen and storage to extend the shelf life of your food, HPG can assist you. It's intriguing to learn that practically all human societies and animals stockpile food. Let's examine the variables impacting food shelf life:

Raw Materials: If a product contains any unprocessed raw materials, the life of the finished product should match the life specified for the raw materials. The reported shelf life of the finished product must be reevaluated if the raw material is cooked or if the criteria vary (for example, a chilled raw material but a frozen final product).

Food safety elements like pH, preservative, water, salt, etc. may be particular to that ingredient and may differ if added in various quantities or may not influence at all similar ingredients. As a result, when combined with other

170

ingredients in a recipe, their reactions may be completely different.

The quantity of ingredients in the recipe may also have an impact on the parameters, which in turn may have an impact on the customer's approval and the food's shelf life.

Packing: Different packing materials may react differently when they come into contact with food, and it's crucial to take into account that chemicals from packaging materials may migrate over time. Dry substances can have their shelf lives increased by using "active" packaging materials like sachets or modified packaging materials.

By completely purging a package of air before closing it, vacuum packaging can increase the life of the goods. The main element in preserving these products is the exclusion of air.

Temperature: The temperature has a significant impact on how long food products stay healthy and safe to eat. The most suitable temperature regimes must be chosen, and they must be used consistently. If you export food, be aware that the conditions for storage are not the same as in your home country. The business-to-consumer supply chain should look into the export process.

Removing moisture from foods before keeping them is advised. For long-term storage, moisture content can only be 10% or less.

Oxygen: Removing oxygen stops the oxidation of dietary ingredients. Oxygen displacement: Use an inert gas (such as nitrogen) to remove air from the product. To remove oxygen, dry ice is frequently employed.

Oxygen absorber: If the oxygen is removed, only 99% pure nitrogen is left because the air already contains 78% nitrogen.

Hygiene: The design and evaluation of products by themselves do not yield enough data to allow for the establishment of a shelf life in relation to food safety.

A few things to think about are as follows:

Building Design: The environments used for handling and storing both food and food contact packaging range from a high-risk environment where contamination by microorganisms is prevented to a low-risk region where the focus is on limiting the growth of germs

Process Design: Because it is impossible for bacteria to grow anywhere other than in the most specialized sectors of food production, it is crucial to develop a thorough understanding of where bacteria are found, how quickly they multiply, and how they contaminate food.

Equipment Design: The less likely any piece of equipment is to be cleaned properly, the harder it is to clean and the longer it takes to clean. Before selecting to introduce equipment to extend the shelf life of food, it is important to understand how often any equipment is used and the techniques employed to prevent equipment recontamination.

Foods react differently after being opened from their packaging, depending on the type. For example, whereas ice cream must be consumed right away, an open packet of chips can be stored for two to three days.

Light has the potential to lower food quality. Therefore, keeping food in dark places is always preferable.

What is Food Shelf Life

To ensure food products are safe, to determine their nutritional value, and to provide instructions for how and when to use, store, and prepare them, food technologists test and analyze food products.

Because food can create the optimal environment for bacteria to develop, it is crucial that food that is ingested be safe to eat. People can become very ill after eating tainted food.

A product's "use-by" date tells you how long you have to eat it before it becomes dangerous; it can be eaten up until and on the date indicated, but it shouldn't be consumed after that. Food safety and use-by dates are related.

A best before date designates the time after which a product's quality and freshness will start to decline. Even though food may still be safe to eat after its best-before date, the texture or flavor may be compromised.

Utilizing tests that measure how long a product maintains its stability under ideal storage circumstances, the shelf life of a product can be determined. The product is continuously examined to determine how long it will be before the standard product deviates from the minimum criteria. The shelf life is shown by this.

The suggested shelf life will only be valid if the suggested conditions are upheld. Some goods will always have a somewhat short shelf life, such as fruit that has been sliced and packaged and ready-made sandwiches or salads.

Food that is ready to consume is also known as high-risk food. Usually, these will have a use-by date attached. Bacteria will thrive in high-risk foods because they offer the right environment.

High-Risk Foods

- Finished rice
- Cooked chicken and meat
- Dairy items (pasteurized milk, cream, and yogurt)
- Seafood, particularly fish.

Low-risk foods are typically high in salt or sugar content, acidic, or have a low water content, and they frequently don't need to be refrigerated before being opened. There will typically be a best before date on these.

Low-Risk Foods

- Vinegars
- Canned goods
- Flour
- Canned pasta
- Honey
- Preserves and jam
- Fresh produce that has not been chopped

UHT milk and pasteurized juices are examples of pasteurized products.

As long as they are properly preserved, frozen foods will have a far longer shelf life than fresh products.

Food that has been frozen shouldn't be refrozen because it won't keep after it's thawed before it loses its suitability for ingestion. Even if frozen food with a longer shelf life isn't necessarily harmful, it will start to lose flavor, texture, or nutritional value.

How to determine the shelf life of food products

The approaches most frequently used today to calculate food's shelf life are:

Direct action

These investigations, which take place in real time, involve storing the product under conditions that are comparable to those it will encounter in the field and tracking its development over time at set intervals.

The primary benefit of this approach is that it generates a very precise estimation of the amount of time it takes for a product to degrade; nevertheless, these studies typically take a long time and do not take into account the fact that a product's storage circumstances are not always constant throughout time.

Trial by Challenge

Using this technique, pathogens or other microorganisms are intentionally introduced into food during production to simulate the circumstances it will face in the wild. The main drawback of this kind of test is that only the effects brought on by the investigated parameters are examined; the possibility that the product may be exposed to many factors concurrently is not taken into account. Additionally, this is research that is tough to implement and highly sophisticated.

Determined microbiology

Based on mathematical and statistical models, this research investigates the various microbial reactions of foods to diverse environmental conditions in order to forecast how the product's microorganisms would behave. This form of study, which is frequently employed when creating new products, does take into account the possibility of a product's conditions altering; however, it has two key drawbacks: it makes the manufacturer's job more complicated, and the results are based on a simulation, which may not be correct.

Quicken shelf life tests

In these tests, conditions such as temperature, oxygen pressure, or moisture content are modified to accelerate the spoilage reactions of a food.

These forecasts enable one to predict how foods will behave under specific circumstances and make predictions about their evolution over time.

Accelerated tests allow for the inclusion of varying environmental circumstances and variations in the ingredient concentrations that make them up. These studies are very adaptable and affordable for the maker, and they enable the comparison of many scenarios. The results are obviously subject to some error because they are not a precise depiction of reality.

Technique of survival

It is a particular kind of research that is focused on the consumer's perception of the physical properties of the product. To ascertain whether they would consume the goods or not, it involves understanding how individuals feel about the same product with various manufacture dates.

By using this technique, it is hoped to link the product's perceived quality with its shelf life. It is crucial to conduct it in addition to other methods to determine a product's best-by date, even though it is not a method to precisely estimate shelf life.

How to calculate shelf life

How to calculate shelf life is shown in the stages below.

1. First, ascertain the date of manufacturing.

2. Determine the expiration date next.

3. Next, put together the equation SL = ED - MD stated earlier.

4. The Shelf Life should then be calculated.

Use the calculator above to verify your answer after entering the variables and computing the outcome.

How to Increase the Shelf Life of Food Products

Meat science has advanced steadily since the beginning of time. Salt, sugar, and smoke were among the earliest meat preservatives.

These techniques haven't lost their appeal despite the invention of refrigeration. Traditional chemical meat preservatives are disappearing, though, as a result of adult customers' increased attention to natural foods.

I. Meat preservatives used by the ancestors

Natural meat preservatives maintain the appearance, smell, and flavor of the food while preventing illness from spoiled food. Even in times of hunger or when hunting is prohibited, humans can always have a reliable source of protein because of meat preservation. Since salt is the earliest known meat preservative, our ancestors have long known to process food in salt in order to preserve it throughout time.

2. Organic Shelf Life Extenders: ACE Ingredients: Aroma

Acearoma is a flavoring product that is primarily based on the normal flavoring components of vinegar and is co-processed with other natural flavoring products to allow for the proper tuning of its mild and round flavor.

Acearoma has the ability to be used in any application involving meat or fish, whether it be raw or cooked, in a brine, or as an ingredient in a powder. Acearoma is a practical and affordable product with clear labeling because of its low applicative dosage. Other preservatives like lactates, lactate/acetate blends, and diacetate can be replaced with it, which has positive impacts on microbiological protection, shelf life, flavor, and cost-saving.

3. How can food products have a longer shelf life?

Food products' shelf lives can be extended throughout the manufacturing process. The environment for microbe development is hampered by decreasing the food's water activity and raising its sugar content.

Another crucial step in extending a product's shelf life is the packaging procedure. High concentrations of CO_2 and N_2 can hinder microorganism growth. Vacuum packing or nitrogen-filled vacuum packaging can therefore increase the shelf life of food.

Another typical technique to extend the shelf life of food is heat treatment, or Jow temperature treatment. Most viruses, yeast, bacteria, and mold nutrient cells can be fatal after 10 minutes at 50 to 60 °C.

Most bacteria cease growing or even die below 0 °C because metabolic reactions cannot occur there. Thus, extending the shelf life of food with heat treatment or low-temperature preservation is successful.

Methods for Increasing Shelf Life

You understand the importance of "shelf life" as the owner of a small food company. There is no denying that the easier it is to ship, store, and sell food, the longer its shelf life. So, in today's blog post, we'd like to teach you six fundamental techniques for extending food's shelf life.

These techniques can be employed individually or in combination to increase sales while extending the biological shelf life of foods.

1. Freeze your product.

Freezing or chilling your product is a simple and arguably the most common approach. This prevents the growth of microorganisms and, when frozen to -18°C, almost completely eradicates them. This may help prevent the growth of bacteria and mold on your merchandise.

2. Heat your item.

Heat is another factor that can kill microbes. In order to prevent them from developing in the first place and to maintain product sterility, "Hot-filling" is an excellent technique. If you produce jams, syrups, and sauces, this technique would be ideal for you.

3. Dried

Drying is a tried-and-true technique for keeping your product safe. Your product's shelf life is greatly increased by removing moisture from it. Free water will become entangled and unavailable to microorganisms if excessive salt and sugar solutions are added to the package. Because of this, jams and marmalades with high sugar content don't need to be refrigerated.

4. Utilizing chemicals

To increase the shelf life of your product, you can combine certain chemicals with some of the other techniques mentioned below. Utilizing oxygen absorbers and antioxidants can lessen oxidation. By being put in several pouches inside a sealed bag, oxygen absorbers have been employed in an indirect manner.

5. Altering the Atmosphere of Your Products

If your product is susceptible to oxidation and is stored in an oxygen-free environment, the degradation has been eliminated. The process known as "Modified Atmosphere Packaging" (MAP) includes adding a gas mixture other than air to a pack, which is then allowed to equilibrate or vary depending on the system's needs.

Vacuum packing, which removes some or all of the oxygen in the container, might be thought of as a form of MAP, but it is not appropriate if your product includes fruits and vegetables because they require air to stay fresh.

6. Product Irradiation

Foods are subjected to ionized radiation during the irradiation process. It is a method that, similar to pasteurizing milk and preserving produce, increases food safety and shelf life by decreasing or removing insects and microorganisms. Irradiation,

when used properly, can be an efficient way to improve the safety of many foods and increase shelf life by eradicating and/or lowering microbial and insect infestations as well as the diseases they cause in your product.

Benefits of Extending Shelf Life

Increasing shelf life has advantages for consumers as well as for manufacturers and enterprises. These include higher profit margins, higher-quality goods, fresher vegetables, and fewer returned items.

A longer shelf life opens up the potential for longer shipments and increases the region that companies can cover.

There are a variety of ways that companies might strive to extend shelf life to decrease food waste, commit to being more sustainable, and boost productivity. Additionally, consumers can empower themselves by making sure they read and comprehend the labels on packages, are aware of the alternatives to chemical additions, and only make purchases from trusted merchants.

Depending on the exact product and how it is offered, a

company may opt for a variety of shelf-life extension strategies.

Businesses involved in the food industry, such as farms, factories, and retailers, will benefit from keeping up with current market trends, cutting-edge scientific research, legislative changes (such as the removal of specific chemical additives), and best practices for increasing shelf life.

Food quality and safety will increase as a result of the development of the food sciences. These advances should, in turn, have an impact on the food manufacturing and retail industries as well as encourage customers to make better decisions. There should be less food waste entering landfills as shelf lives for products are extended.

CONCLUSION

In conclusion, Ball canning is a time-tested and reliable method for preserving and storing food. With a rich history dating back to the late 19th century, Ball canning jars have become an iconic symbol of home food preservation.

Throughout the years, Ball has not only provided high-quality canning jars but also developed a comprehensive range of canning equipment and resources to support and educate home canners. From pressure canners and water bath canners to canning accessories and recipe guides, Ball has continuously strived to make the canning process accessible and enjoyable for everyone.

By using the Ball canning method, individuals can extend the shelf life of their favorite fruits, vegetables, jams, jellies, pickles, and more. The process ensures that the natural flavors, textures, and nutrients of the food are preserved, allowing individuals to savor the tastes of the season long after they are harvested.

Moreover, Ball canning promotes sustainable practices by reducing food waste and supporting local and seasonal eating. It empowers individuals to take control of their food supply, providing a sense of satisfaction and self-reliance.

Furthermore, the versatility of Ball canning extends beyond food preservation. The iconic Mason jars have become popular for various creative purposes, such as crafting, organizing, and even serving food and beverages. Their timeless design and durability make them a beloved staple in many households.

In a world where convenience and mass production dominate, Ball canning offers a return to simpler times, where individuals can connect with their food and create lasting memories. It fosters a sense of tradition and an appreciation for the bounty of nature.

In summary, Ball canning is a testament to the enduring value of preserving food at home. It combines innovation, tradition, and quality to empower individuals in their culinary pursuits. Whether you are an experienced canner or just starting out, Ball provides the tools and knowledge to embark on a rewarding journey of food preservation. Embrace the art of canning and enjoy the flavors of nature all year round with Ball.

Here are the steps in a nutshell:

1. Understand the basics of ball canning.

2. Choose a method of canning (water bath or pressure canning).

3. Follow a step-by-step guide for the method you have chosen.

4. Process the jars in the water bath or pressure canner.

5. Cool, store, and check the seals of the jars.

By following these steps, you can be sure that your canned food is safe and delicious.

Made in the USA
Monee, IL
20 August 2023